THE WORLD'S MOST EVIL GANGSTERS

THE WORLD'S MOST EVIL GANGSTERS

NIGEL CAWTHORNE

JOHN BLAKE

Published by John Blake Publishing Ltd,
3 Bramber Court, 2 Bramber Road,
London W14 9PB, England

www.johnblakepublishing.co.uk

First published in paperback, 2010

ISBN: 978 1 84454 957 3

British Library Cataloguing-in-Publication Data:

A catalogue record for this book is available from the British Library.

Design by www.envydesign.co.uk

Printed in Great Britain by CPI Bookmarque, Croydon CR0 4TD

1 3 5 7 9 10 8 6 4 2

Papers used by John Blake Publishing are natural, recyclable products
made from wood grown in sustainable forests. The manufacturing processes
conform to the environmental regulations of the country of origin.

CONTENTS

INTRODUCTION   VII

CHAPTER 1:   **THE PECKHAM BOYS**   1

CHAPTER 2:   **TAMIL SNAKE GANG**   27

CHAPTER 3:   **THE GOOCHES AND THE DODDINGTONS**   43

CHAPTER 4:   **THE ESSEX BOYS**   73

CHAPTER 5:   **THE YARDIES**   93

CHAPTER 6:   **THE AGGI CREW**   129

CHAPTER 7:   **THE BURGER BAR BOYS**   139

CHAPTER 8:   **THE POLLOKSHIELDS PAKISTANI MAFIA**   175

CHAPTER 9:   **THE PETTINGILL FAMILY**   189

CHAPTER 10: **THE MORANS**   201

CHAPTER 11: **THE BLOODS AND THE LUCCHESES**   213

CHAPTER 12: **THE CRIPS**   231

CONTENTS

INTRODUCTION

Gangsta rap is out there, along with gangsta movies – *Boyz n the Hood, Menace II Society*. The 'gangsta' style has spread from South Los Angeles, inspiring inner-city youth across the world. For the most part, this is harmless. The progenitors of gangsta rap – Ice-T, N.W.A., Snoop Doggy Dogg – are wealthy and have no reason to resort to crime. Indeed they are positively inspirational, demonstrating that it is possible to take the gritty reality of inner-city life, crime, violence, sexual exploitation and racial prejudice and turn them into gold – bling, indeed. There is a way out of the ghetto. Snoop Dogg has gone platinum four times and makes more money than the president.

However, there are those more wedded to the gansta creed. There are groups of disaffected youth who see no life beyond drug dealing, pimping and armed robbery. They win their spurs with senseless acts of violence and have no qualms about killing. They intend to live fast and die young. Sadly, this is often their fate. Alternatively, they face a few brief years of mindless fun then a vast stretch of their adult life – if not all of it – behind bars. Even in jurisdictions where they have the death penalty, the convict usually has to spend long years on death row contemplating the inevitable – and even having a change of heart – while the process of appeal grinds on to exhaustion.

London has always had its fair share of gangs. Some of the historic outfits have a very modern ring to them. In the late sixteenth and early seventeenth century, there was the Damned Crew, also known as the Cursed Crew. They were noted for swaggering around the streets, the worse for drink, and assaulting watchmen and passers-by. Having no hoods, they pulled their hats down over their eyes. Their leader was Edmund Baynham. On the night of Tuesday 18 March 1600, Baynham and his crew left the Mermaid tavern at midnight and set off apparently looking for trouble. They 'cast off their cloaks and upper garments, drew rapiers' – the AK-47s of the day – 'and daggers, marched through the streets'. When challenged by the watch, they attacked and, after a scuffle, were overpowered. Disarmed, they were marched to prison with Baynham shouting that he 'cared not a fart for the Lord Mayor or any magistrate in London.' Instead of being tried by the ordinary London authorities, however, they were remitted to Star Chamber on the personal intervention of Elizabeth I, 'for the more exemplar punishment of so great and outrageous disorder'. Having at first denied the charges they changed their plea and 'confessed their faults and submitted themselves to the court, and proved that all was done in drink and heat'. They were fined £200 and imprisoned. As a result, a satirical poem was written by Samuel Rowlands about the Damned Crew called *The Letting of Humour's Blood in the Head-vaine* – a kind of Elizabethan gangsta rap. Baynham, a disaffected Catholic, was later implicated in the Essex rebellion and the Gunpowder Plot.

After the Restoration in 1660, gangs proliferated. The historian Thomas Macaulay wrote of the dangers of walking the streets of London's West End.

'When the evening closed in, the difficulty and danger of walking about London became serious indeed. The garret windows were opened and pails were emptied, with little regard to those who were passing below. Falls, bruises and broken bones were of constant occurrence; for, till the last year of the reign of Charles II, most of the streets were left in profound darkness. Thieves and robbers plied their trade with impunity; yet they were hardly so terrible to peaceful citizens as another class of ruffians. It was a favourite amusement of dissolute young gentlemen to swagger by night about the town, breaking windows, upsetting sedans, beating quiet men, and offering rude caresses to pretty women. Several dynasties of these tyrants had, since the Restoration, domineered over the streets. The "Muns" and "Tityre Tus" had given place to the "Hectors", and the "Hectors" had been recently succeeded by the "Scourers". At a later period arose the "Nicker", the "Hawcubite", and the yet more dreaded name of "Mohawk", as we learn from Oldham's "Imitation of the Third Satire of Juvenal" (1682), and Shadwell's "Scourers" (1690).'

Macaulay continued: 'Many other authorities will

readily occur to all who are acquainted with the popular literature of that and the succeeding generation. It may be suspected that some of the "Tityre Tus", like good Cavaliers, broke Milton's windows shortly after the Restoration. I am confident that he was thinking of those pests of London when he dictated the noble lines:

And in luxurious cities, where the noise
Of riot ascends above their loftiest towers,
And injury and outrage, and when night
Darkens the streets, then wander forth the sons
Of Belial, flown with insolence and wine.

Elsewhere, the Mohawks are called the 'Mohocks', but took their name from the Mohawk Indians, in either case. They were also known as 'young bloods' – or just the 'bloods', like the modern-day American gang. They sexually molested women and disfigured men. According to Lady Wentworth: 'They put an old woman into a hogshead, and rolled her down a hill; they cut off some noses, others' hands, and several barbarous tricks, without any provocation. They are said to be young gentlemen; they never take any money from any.'

Their leader was known as 'The Emperor of the Mohocks' and was distinguished by a crescent tattoo on his forehead. Tattoos are very gangsta.

In the nineteenth century 'hooligans' ran wild. Their name is thought to have derived from 'Hooley's gang'. The 1930s were another golden age for London gangsters, but many of them were Sicilians who found themselves interned during World War II and later deported, leaving room for home-grown gangsters that spawned the Krays, the Richardsons and the other gangs of the 1960s.

That generation of gangsters are long gone. The new crop carry sub-machine guns. They commit murderous acts of violence on a whim or to gain 'respeck' and they do not care whose blood is shed. These gangs exist in most major cities in the UK. Two of the gangs in south Manchester, the Gooch and Doddington gangs, began such a violent turf war that representatives of the American Crips and the Bloods – who had a truce at the time, as their drug distribution empires spread out across the US – flew over from Los Angeles to broker a ceasefire.

Currently, the police believe that there are more than 250 gangs in London alone. Some of have an ethnic base – Somali, Tamil, Pakistani. Then there are the Yardies, whose members were brought up amid the murderous political rivalries of Jamaica and have killed many times before they arrive in Britain.

Australia has its own gangster culture. This was most vividly portrayed in the 13-part Australian TV series *Underbelly*, which dramatised the gangland war in Melbourne, lasting from 1995 to 2004. Australia also has a growing problem with ethnic gangs, particularly second and third generation Lebanese.

Areas of the city centres in the UK, US and Oz have turned into the Wild West. Knives flash and bullets fly. The innocent get hit in the crossfire, but the good guys rarely get a look in.

Who is to say who are the most evil gangsters in the world? I have picked 12 gangs whose members care nothing for anyone's life, least of all their own, and have no regard for the effect they have on the rest of society. They force those around them to live in fear. Decent people are cowed into silence. The weak are corrupted with drugs; women are forced into prostitution and youngsters are encouraged to emulate their vicious ways. This affects us all and is evil by any definition.

Nigel Cawthorne
Bloomsbury, July 2010

CHAPTER 1

THE PECKHAM BOYS

The Peckham Boys had been on the streets for around a decade before the murder of Damilola Taylor in November 2000. However, the senseless murder of an innocent ten-year-old brought them into the headlines. Born in Lagos, Damilola had only arrived in the United Kingdom with his family in August 2000 so his sister Gbemi could be treated for epilepsy. They were staying with relatives on the North Peckham Estate. Knowing nothing of the area, they thought they were safe.

Damilola went to a local school, Oliver Goldsmith Primary, in Camberwell. Teachers there were impressed by his ability and his enthusiasm. The headmaster, Mark Parsons, said: 'He was slowly making friends and settling into the school. He was a boisterous, fun, smiling boy. If I think about him, I think of him smiling.'

However, there were signs that the new boy was being bullied. On Friday 24 November, three days before his death, he told his mother Gloria he was being called names and had been beaten up.

'Damilola came home on Friday night and said he had been beaten,' she said. 'I asked, "Did you fight with them?" and he said, "No mummy, I did not fight with them." He said he was in pain.'

Mrs Taylor was so concerned that, at the first opportunity on Monday morning, she escorted her son to school to talk to Mr Parsons about the older boys who were bullying Damilola.

'They were calling him names and saying things like "fuck your mother",' she said. 'He asked me, "Mummy, what is the meaning of gay?" These boys were calling him gay and I said, "Do not listen to them." I said, "Go and report it to the school teacher," and when he came home he said he reported it but the teacher did not know who was telling the truth.'

Damilola had signed up with a computer club in Peckham Library where he would go most days straight after school. On Monday, 27 November, he left the library at 4.30pm, to make his way home. This was captured on CCTV. As he approached the North Peckham Estate, he was grabbed by three hooded youths dressed in dark clothing, who held him a headlock and stabbed him in the left thigh. This is a punishment known as 'juking' and it is usually used on anyone who dares to defend themselves.

Bleeding heavily from his severed femoral artery, Damilola staggered a hundred yards. Finding sanctuary in a stairwell near his home, he collapsed in a pool of blood. A member of the public who found Damilola barely conscious on a first-floor stairwell at 4.50pm called the emergency services. Paramedics carried out emergency treatment, but the boy was dead on arrival at King's College Hospital in Camberwell. Two kitchen knives and a bloodstained broken bottle were found in the vicinity.

From the beginning, the police were aware there were local youths who knew who the killer was, but they were blocked at every turn. Gang culture in the area was so strong that no one would speak out against them. The mother of a boy arrested in connection with Damilola's murder but not charged, recalled: 'We were in the police station interview room, and I asked him if he had killed Damilola. He said no. I asked him if he knew who did, and he said yes. I told him to tell the police, and he looked at me as if I was mad. Then he said: "I ain't no grass." It was like something out of a bad gangster film.'

As far as she knew, her son was not a member of a gang.

'He'd never been in any trouble,' she said. 'I thought he was a good boy, but he was still caught up in the culture.'

This level of intransigence was something the police were totally unprepared for.

'When I first started, you'd sometimes stick kids in a cell just to show them what it was like,' said one retired detective. 'It used to scare the shit out of them. If you tried that these days the only thing that would happen would be that the kid's street cred would go up. And then you'd get a writ for unlawful imprisonment. I've arrested 11-year-olds who have been as calm as anything, and just handed over the card of their solicitor and told me they won't say a word until their brief arrives. It's unbelievable. It's like dealing with someone whose been in the game for decades.'

Detective Superintendent Trevor Shepherd, the senior

officer in the Damilola murder hunt, encountered this first hand when his team hit the streets to seek information.

'The loyalty of these youngsters to each other was very difficult for us to break down,' he said. 'Their lives revolve around being on the streets and having the respect of their friends. Nothing else matters.'

The only person to break ranks during the investigation was a 14-year-old girl, known by the codename 'Bromley', who claimed to have seen the murder take place. In 2002, four youths, including two 16-year-old brothers, went on trial at the Old Bailey for the murder of Damilola Taylor. But during the trial, when videos of her police interviews were shown, the jury were shocked to see her singing and joking about the £50,000 reward she hoped to collect. Carolyn Crooks, the officer who interviewed her, was accused of 'inducing' Bromley to change her story in order to get the reward money. Bromley eventually admitted lying in some of her evidence, and the judge told the jury to disregard her entire testimony. Two of the defendants were then discharged by the judge. The other two were acquitted by the jury. Bromley was given psychiatric help and sent to live under the Witness Protection Programme.

Three years later, new DNA techniques led to a re-examination of the evidence. In 2005, 19-year-old Hassan Jihad was arrest, along with two brothers aged 16 and 17 who could not be named at the time because of their age. On 23 January 2006 Hassan Jihad was acquitted and, although the two brothers were found not guilty on the murder charge, the jury could not decide whether they had committed manslaughter. At a retrial, they were convicted.

By then, they were both 18 and could be named. Their

names were Ricky Gavin Preddie and Danny Charles Preddie. When the verdict was given, Ricky Preddie had to be dragged away by prison service officers after swearing at the court and shouting, 'You're all going to pay for this.' The judge, Mr Justice Goldring, ordered, 'Take him down.' After a brief pause, when the shouting from the cells below could still be heard in court, he added, 'Take him right down.' The two brothers were each sentenced to eight years' imprisonment.

The Preddie brothers were members of the Young Peckham Boys, a group of youths affiliated to the main gang. They were only 12 and 13 at the time of the murder. A policeman who worked in Peckham at the time of Damilola's death described the two boys as 'the scum of the earth'.

'Whenever there was a robbery, one or other of the Preddies was involved,' he said.

The Young Peckham Boys were terrorising the North Peckham Estate when Damilola was killed. It was said that they would knife you in the blink of an eye just to show how tough they were. At the time, the Preddies had not graduated into the Peckham Boys proper, whose elite teenage members sleep with 'Baby Nines' – 9mm pistols – under their pillows and compete for the respect of their peers with their crimes. However, on 27 November 2000, they gained the 'ultimate respect'. The murder of ten-year-old Damilola turned them into local heroes.

The Preddies luxuriated in their new-found fame and scoffed as the police struggled to find Damilola's killers. Ex-gang member 'Steve' said: 'The Preddies feared nobody and used brute violence to earn respect. By the time the police finally sent them down they had become heroes to kids on the street.'

In January 2001, just weeks after they had killed Damilola, they led a mob on to a packed commuter train at London Bridge railway station during rush hour.

'We called it "gauging" and it was what the Preddies loved to do,' said Steve. 'You'd steam on and grab handbags and wallets. This night, a guy about 40 put up a fight – but Danny cracked him with a knuckleduster and Ricky jumped from a chair on to his head. I thought he was dead. As we ran off, Ricky grabbed a £5 watch off his wrist and asked Danny if he heard his jaw break. They were obsessed with violence.'

The Preddies' father, Alfred, was a boxer from Jamaica who was notorious in the area for siring 20 kids by different women before he died in 2004. Born in Lambeth, the Preddie brothers had been brought up in Peckham by their mother Marion, a fiery woman of Jamaican origin. Steve met the brothers in 1994 when they attended Gloucester Grove Primary School together.

'Even at seven and eight, they were bringing in fat joints of cannabis to school and passing them round,' he said. 'All through those years dope fuelled us. We smoked it from noon until midnight. We went to bed stoned and woke up raging and ready to steal. People say it's harmless, but we couldn't live without it.'

They dropped out of school and were left to fend for themselves. Steve and the Preddies signed up to the Peckham Boys in 1997 when they were ten.

'For the first time in our lives we had a little bit of respect,' said Steve. 'But we had to earn it.'

At the time, the Peckham Boys were over a hundred strong. Members were split into three ranks – the Elders, the Youngers and the Tinys or Kidz. An inner circle of Elders controlled the gang and the smaller boys earned their respect by getting 'rowdy' – that is, mugging a passer-by or committing a random act of violence on someone for absolutely no reason. The Preddies were members of the Younger Peckham Boys and liked being referred to as 'soldiers'. They loved the mindless brutality. They would join in the 'bang-for-bang' games where they had to stand toe-to-toe with an older gang member and trade punches until one was knocked unconscious. Soon they virtually controlled the Gloucester Grove housing estate and the North Peckham Estate where Damilola died.

As well as indulging their taste for blood, the Preddies became tireless thieves.

'The Elders saw them as good earners,' said Steve. 'They were fearless. The Preddies would attack anyone but would go out of the estates and target people in suits, with laptops, with nice bags. They quickly got a good rep [reputation].'

However, to climb the gang's hierarchy, Ricky and Danny would have to show a greater dedication to violence. One way to do that was to do a little 'juking' – stabbing someone in the arm or leg at random. The idea was to cause serious injury, but not actually to kill anyone.

When the Preddies saw Damilola skipping home from school, he was, to them, an obvious target – not someone who was likely to put up much resistance.

'We all knew Damilola but not well,' said Steve. 'He was the happy kid who always seemed to be smiling.'

After Damilola was killed, people said he'd been bullied

by the Peckham Boys, but Steve said that was not true. The attack was a one-off.

'Each time I saw him I thought he looked like a good kid,' he said, 'a million miles from the life we were living: mugging, smoking weed, stealing cars. I think he was targeted because he didn't lead that life.'

Steve believed the Preddies did not mean to kill Damilola. But juking him was an obvious career move.

'Stabbing gives you a higher rep on the street,' he said. 'That's what the Preddies wanted.'

Five days after Damilola's death Ricky and Danny were arrested on suspicion of his murder. When the police bungled the Damilola murder investigation, the brothers walked free – only increasing their reputation in south London. Now the Preddies were top dogs and they went on a crime spree.

While Ricky and Danny Preddie were carrying out these crimes, the police were otherwise engaged. One hundred-and-twenty of them were involved in Operation Seale, searching for the killer of Damilola Taylor. No only did they meet with a wall of silence, they came across a new breed of feral children on the streets who ran wild, looking for sex and drugs, and had no fear of the law.

Calling themselves Ruff Riders, the Ghetto Boys, the Firehouse Crew and the notorious Peckham Boys, these kids met at night and roamed in packs. They listened to gangsta rap and idolised the heroes of films like *Goodfellas*, *Scarface* and *Menace II Society*, aping their language and adopting their values. They talked about people getting 'jacked' – mugged or robbed – and being 'blazed' – or shot. These kids said they wanted 'the Cris life', a reference to Cristal champagne, the ultimate in underworld chic. To them, their street confrontations were unscripted drama performances that they improvised. The street was their stage where they acted out roles.

To the Peckham Boys, the police were the enemy. The worst thing anyone could possibly do was co-operate with them. Ten days after the murder of Damilola, a scrawny, pockmarked 14-year-old was taken into Edmonton police station. Because of his age, social workers were present at the interview along with the boy's lawyers. While a detective constable asked him about the killing, without warning, the boy leapt forward and viciously head-butted the officer, smashing his nose. The detective reeled backwards with blood cascading down his face.

'Well?' sneered the teenager, folding his arms across his chest. 'What you going to do about that?'

Ricky and Danny Preddie worked independently. However, they planned their crimes together and then went their separate ways with their own crews. Later they would meet to compare hauls. Steve said they were very close and never fought each other. Over ten years Steve reckoned they made £250,000, though the Peckham Boys' Elders took a cut of everything they stole. They always wore the best tracksuits and had a new gold chain every week. And they rarely went home to their mum. At night they preferred to stay with the girls they had all over Peckham.

Steve reckoned that the botched police investigation into Damilola's death that dragged on for six years helped empower gangs like the Peckham Boys on the streets. During the investigation the police repeatedly bumped into the Preddies. In December 2002, Ricky was prosecuted after throwing a bottle at another youth. In 2005, he was sentenced to 12 months' detention for driving while disqualified, assault and other offences.

Danny was also in custody when they were charged with Damilola's murder. In March 2006, he was sentenced to three years detention at Inner London Crown Court for conspiracy to commit robbery. He had been part of a 'steaming gang' that was robbing rail passengers. He threatened to cut one victim's face before stealing £5. Another passenger had a knife pushed against his stomach while his mobile phone and £15 in cash was stolen by the gang.

After three trials, it was only in October 2006 that Ricky and Danny Preddie were jailed for Damilola's death. At the trial, prosecutors said the Preddies wanted to be London's most feared gangsters 'like the Kray twins'. Steve confirmed this.

'They aimed to be the top boys just like the Krays had been,' he said.

They were sentenced to just eight years for manslaughter. In a final act of defiance, the Preddies sneered, yelled and raised their hands as they were taken down.

Damilola's parents, Richard and Gloria, condemned the light sentence. With parole and time already spent on remand, the Preddies could be back on the streets in three years.

'We question whether these sentences will act as an appropriate deterrent,' said Richard Taylor. 'We believe Damilola's murder reflects a crisis within our communities which is now out of control.'

Although the killing of Damilola Taylor brought the

existence of the Peckham Boys to national attention, the history of the Peckham Boys and other Peckham gangs can be traced back decades to fights between pupils from Peckham, Brixton and Lewisham that erupted at the Kingsdale School in the 1950s. These were caused by the changing demographics of the area. During World War II, the once wealthy area of Brixton had been heavily bombed, so new housing estates were built there. Many rich people moved out, leaving their large terraced houses to be divided up into multi-occupancy dwellings with as many as five families living in each. Most kids from Brixton were sent to Kingsdale School in the relatively posh area of Sydenham, as the residents there tended to send their children to private – and public – schools, leaving local schools relatively under-attended. Kids from Peckham and other poor areas were also sent there. This caused cultural clashes between what grew to be a predominantly African, particularly Nigerian, community in Peckham with neighbouring Caribbean communities in New Cross, Deptford, Brockley and Brixton. The Brixton boys and Peckham lads used to fight every day, and there were countless campaigns by local residents to shut the school down, especially when the gangs started picking on the kids from the local private schools.

These gangs became established and, over the next 50 years, new generations periodically replaced older members. And with each new generation they changed their names. Back in the 1970s, in Peckham there were the Gloucester Grove Boys, the Night Jackyls and the Untouchables. Throughout the 1980s and into the 1990s there were North Peckham Boys, Yellow Brick Massive,

Peckham Grove Boys, Outlaws and Acorn Crew – all from the estates within Peckham and the SE15 area.

Since the mid-1990s, there has been a consolidation of the Peckham Boys in SE15. The main gang was Peckham Boy Gangstaz, a multiracial gang made up of young men over 18. There were the Younger Peckham Boyz, made up of kids between the ages of 14 and 18 who would one day graduate into Peckham Boy Gangstaz. Then there were the Tiny Peckham Boyz, made up of kids under 14. The gang was spread around Peckham, notably on the Gloucester Grove, North Peckham, Goldsmiths and Penthouse Estates. Alongside them were the Acorn Boyz, an all-black gang from Acorn Estate on Queen's Road. They were probably the most hated of all the factions.

There were a number of cliques within the Peckham Boys, headed by a dozen older, well-established members known as the Elders. Although the gang has become more racially mixed than it was in the 1960s, it retains a rigid command structure that some have compared to the Mafia. The Elders provided knives and guns, and controlled the teams of fearless young thugs who brought in a regular stream of stolen cash and valuables. Their influence spread from Peckham into other areas such as Walworth Road's Browning and Heygate estates, home of the Peckham Boys' infamous allies, the Firehouse Crew. They were mostly Nigerian, aged between 16 and 25, along with some mixed-race young men. Then there were the Moneymakaz, a break-off from the Firehouse Crew, comprising mostly mixed-race kids from the Sumner Estate. They found themselves on the front line against white racist gangs including the Nunhead National Front – Nunhead lies directly south of Peckham. The Nunhead NF were aligned with the Eltham NF and Bermondsey Boyz, and wore blue, the colour of Millwall football club.

In 1987, because of the amount of robbery, violent crime and youth gangs in the area, Prime Minister Margaret Thatcher earmarked North Peckham for regeneration. She set up a taskforce. Over £1 million was spent, but none of the problems were solved. In the summer of 2000 an 18-year-old girl was shot outside a nightclub on the 'frontline' in Brixton, while an African restaurant used by older Peckham Boys was raided by police who recovered a .357 handgun, a stun gun, CS gas and cannabis. A few weeks later a Young Peckham Boy, aged 12, appeared in court after being found in possession of heroin, crack and £400 in cash. A gun battle outside Chicago's nightclub on the frontline saw eight people wounded. Then in November, just nine days before the killing of Damilola Taylor, 17-year-old Shola Agora of Sceaux Gardens estate in Southwark was stabbed, and later died at King's College Hospital.

After the death of Damilola the building where he was killed was knocked down. The rundown high-rise flats around it have been replaced with two thousand new homes, a sports and leisure centre and an award-winning library at a cost of £290 million. Despite this, the gangs and violence remain.

By the time the Preddies were convicted, there was a gang war going on between the Peckham Boys and their rivals the Ghetto Boys, from nearby New Cross. Ghetto and Peckham had never got on. There had always been a clash between the African contingent of Peckham, from the main gang areas of north Peckham, and the Caribbean contingent from New Cross, Deptford and Brockley. Even local football matches between Peckham and Lewisham teams would be highly charged.

A Ghetto Boy told journalist Donal MacIntyre: 'If any of those Peckham Boys come over to New Cross, this will happen.' And he ran his finger across his throat. MacIntyre asked if the war between the Ghetto Boys and the 'Pecknarm' – the slang name for Peckham – was about drugs. He was told that the rivalry between the two gangs was inherited, not drugs or turf related. It had been going on since the 1970s and was handed down by gangsters from generation to generation.

In March 2001 the Peckham Boys went to a So Solid Crew concert at Atmospheres Nightclub in Luton, but were refused entry, though some of them managed to get in. When the event ended at 2am, people leaving the area found their way blocked by cars, and there were several confrontations. A running battle broke out. It started in Flowers Way and moved into Park Street West. In Chapel Street the Peckham Boys became involved in a fight with another group. Both sides were armed. Eighteen-year-old student Marcus Hall, from Peckham, was carrying a baseball bat. It did him no good. During the fight, Hall was stabbed and beaten to death. Four men were convicted of his murder at the Old Bailey in July 2002, but two years later two of them were freed by the Court of Appeal.

A Peckham Boy was stabbed to death outside a McDonalds drive-through in Malt Street, off the Old Kent Road, at around 10pm on 10 September 2003. A murder investigation was set up, but police received little response and the CCTV images were too poor to see the suspects. However, after a specialist review of the CCTV it appeared the victim was touched on his shoulder by one of his attackers. DNA taken from the victim's jumper where he had been touched led police to a suspect.

In July 2004 former gang member Eric Akinniranye was chased and gunned down. He had recently been released on temporary licence from prison where he had been serving ten years for drugs and firearms offences. At the time he was riding a motorcycle along Camberwell High Street when two gunmen in a Mercedes four-by-four rammed him. He tried to escape, but they brought him down with a number of shots. Then they shot him point-blank as he lay on the road. The murder took place in broad daylight in full view of two crowded buses and a street full of onlookers.

Peckham Boys and Ghetto Boys clashed again outside the Urban Music Awards at the Barbican in November 2004. Eighteen shots were fired as people left the awards ceremony. One stray bullet struck an innocent bystander – 25-year-old Helen Kelly. Luckily, it hit the underwire of her bra, deflecting the bullet away from her chest and into her right breast. She collapsed, covered in blood, and thought she was dying.

'I heard some bangs but I didn't think it was gunfire,' she said. 'I started running. Then I looked down and saw blood on my stomach and it was only then I realised I had been shot. I'm still not sure how it happened, but the underwire on my bra snapped when the bullet hit it and I think it did stop it going any further.'

Twenty-eight-year-old Linton Ambursley from

Lewisham was jailed for 12 years after admitting wounding with intent. Tyrone Headley, also 28, from New Cross, was jailed for two years for assisting an offender.

More recently, the distinction between Peckham Boys, Young Peckham Boys, Tinyz and so on has become redundant as the gang culture and age demographic has shifted into a new generation. These days the gang is becoming more commonly referred to as the Black Gang, with numerous cliques such as SN1 (Spare No-1), SI (Shoot Instantly) and DFA (Don't Fuck Around). Then there are the Shower Crew and the Pelican Crew.

These young gangsters spend their day in school. But when they come home in the evening they put on the uniform of the street. They come out like actors, transformed from schoolboys into gangsters. Typically, street uniform comprises designer sports gear with hoods and basketball caps. The youngsters gather on the estate as the criminal activities of the night unfold. The government's efforts to control knives and guns has made little difference to them as weapons can be fashioned out of almost anything to hand. Many youngsters stash bricks and planks at certain places around the estate in case they are needed. Others carry baseball bats and CS gas.

In June 2006, masked intruders in hooded tops burst into a christening in Peckham. One of the guests, Zainab Kalokoh, died from a single shot to the head as she cradled the baby. The gang stole handbags, mobile phones and wine before fleeing. This time the perpetrators were caught almost immediately. They were aged 14, 16 and 17.

By 2006, the 'don' of the Peckham Boys was said to be Knuckles, a feared bare-knuckle fighter. Then there was

25-year-old Marlon Grandison, who claimed to be their 'commander in chief'. The street posses Grandison headed were linked to dozens of crimes. The police stopped him in Peckham in July 2006. In a black rucksack in the boot of his Fiat Punto, they found a Mac-10 machine pistol, three Baikal Makarov pistols, 62 hollow-point bullets, 379 rounds of ammunition, two silencers, gunpowder, a block of cocaine worth more than £5,000, a balaclava, gloves and fake ecstasy tablets. Traces of his blood were found on the Mac-10. It was thought that he accidentally wounded himself. Ballistics tests linked the three pistols to six unsolved shooting incidents but police could not produce evidence in court that Grandison had fired the weapons. In September 2007 he was sentenced to life for possessing firearms and ammunition. He must serve a minimum of ten years in jail before he can be considered for parole. Grandison's mother, who watched from the public gallery, shouted 'Head up, Marlon' as he was led away to begin his sentence.

In August 2006, a 16-year-old boy was stabbed opposite a bookmakers in New Cross. Another 16-year-old was charged with attempted murder. Then in September 2006, the Ghetto Boys carried out two drive-by shootings in Peckham. Only days later two teenagers were shot in a McDonald's in Brixton in what was thought to have been an act of retaliation. Soon after, the Peckham Boys rampaged through the Ghetto Boys' territory in New Cross. It seems they had clashed at a party, accusing one another of showing disrespect. Things turned nasty when one man was bottled. Twenty-four hours later up to 40 gang members from Peckham armed with knives and a gas-gun rode on bikes into the Woodpecker Estate in New Cross, home turf of the Ghetto Boys. Twenty-nine-year-old Jason Gale-Bent was sitting with his brother and another friend on a wall just yards from their home in Ludwick Mews. Ten years earlier Jason had been a Ghetto Boy, but he had been stabbed and had had to be airlifted to hospital for emergency treatment. This experience convinced him to shun the gangs and gangland violence that permeates south London. At about 9pm, a gang of more than 30 youths on mountain bikes appeared in the street. One of them pulled out a gun and started firing. A fight followed during which Jason was stabbed in the heart. He managed to stagger about 30 yards to his home where he collapsed and died. It was thought he had been mistaken for a member of the gang. At the time of his death he was working as a labourer and looking for a flat to share with his girlfriend. A second man had also been stabbed.

His mother, Eileen Gale, issued a statement for the family, saying: 'Jason was a friendly person who did not associate himself with any particular group and was not a member of any gang. There is nothing that can be done to bring him back to me. I abhor violence and ask that as a community we work towards bringing Jason's killers to justice. No other mother should have to suffer like I am.'

Shortly after Jason's murder a large group of youths on bicycles appeared outside the Community Action Centre in Deptford. A gun was fired and a man on a moped was chased by the youths. He crashed and tried to make off on foot. They caught him and stabbed him in a doorway.

The following evening, a 16-year-old youth and two men, aged 21 and 28, were playing football on a basketball court in Peckham when a car pulled up. Three men in hooded tops got out and shouted: 'Peckham Boys are pussies.' Then they pointed a gun through the railings and fired three shots. No one was injured. Hours later police raided a property in Peckham and arrested a man and a 17-year-old girl, and seized a Walther PPK pistol, a Mac-10, ammunition and some Class A drugs. But the police didn't think this was going to be the end of the matter. Fearing further drive-by shootings, police evacuated two nearby schools.

The authorities were finding themselves increasingly powerless to stop explosions of gang violence; the gangs simply laughed at the police.

'Why wouldn't they?' said Steve, who had quit the Peckham Boys. 'They took years to solve the [Damilola Taylor] case and Danny and Ricky became heroes. They could both be out within three years. What kind of message does that send out?'

Steve regretted the time he had spent with the gang. In October 2006, he spoke to the *Sunday Mirror* in the hope he could warn others of the dangers of youth gangs.

'We went from kids to trained, sophisticated criminals,' he said, 'and we learned everything from the street. We were trained by our peers not to fear violence but to use it. When we needed money, we went out robbing. If we wanted a girl, there was one across the street an Elder would give us. If people feared you, you had it all... But I saw sense. I took a step back and realised I didn't want to be a part of that.'

Steve remains convinced that the Preddies will still be considered heroes when they are released.

'I was chatting to an old pal who is still in the Boys,' he said. 'He said there are kids walking around saying they want to be the next Danny or Ricky. For me, that's the biggest tragedy of all.'

Meanwhile, the litany of murder continues. In February 2007, 21-one-year-old Javarie Crighton was killed not two hundred yards from where Damilola died. Along with Orando Madden, Mohammed Sannoh and Hakeem Dosunmu he had been involved in a number of armed robberies of security guards delivering or collecting money from banks, building societies and supermarkets across south London. Although they were taking Peckham gangland crime to a new level, the robberies were unsophisticated and involved very little planning. The gang would keep watch on a particular bank or building society. Then one of them would then rob the security guards at gunpoint. Afterwards, they would share the proceeds.

The haul was never huge – £25,000 was their biggest payday. Their last robbery netted £18,000, but in one raid they took only £1,000. In another, they got nothing at all because the cash box was booby-trapped, rigged to destroy the money inside. This made the gang suspicious of 24-year-old Madden, the triggerman on that job. When he said the box was empty, they claimed he had ripped them off.

On 3 February, Crighton and Sannoh confronted Madden outside his home in Peckham and demanded their share. Madden lost his temper and stabbed Crighton to death before running away. A few days later he handed himself in to the police, claiming he had killed in self-defence.

Unable to get at Madden, 19-year-old Sannoh sought to avenge his friend by targeting Madden's right-hand man,

Hakeem Dosunmu, who he believed had been looking after the proceeds of the robbery for Madden. He recruited his friend, 22-year-old Abdi Omar Noor, a member of the Pelican Crew. In the early hours of 6 February, they burst into the maisonette in Diamond Street, Peckham, where Dosunmu lived with his parents, his sister Shakira and his younger brother Michael. It was just 200 yards from where Crighton had been killed. The two gunmen ran upstairs and into a bedroom, where they fired a burst of eight shots from a Mac-10 sub-machine gun. Three of them hit 15-year-old schoolboy Michael, who lay in bed asleep. Hakeem was out at the time. His mother was away visiting relatives in Nigeria and his father Rasak, a senior psychiatric nurse, was in hospital after suffering a fall. Michael died in the arms of his older sister.

University student Shakira told police she had been woken by gunfire and saw a man wearing an army jacket, his face hidden by a scarf. After the pair fled she discovered her brother's body still wrapped up in his duvet. She tried to resuscitate him. But one of the bullets had pierced his heart, killing him. A devout Christian, Michael had been a regular communicant at the nearby Celestial Church of Christ, and wanted to become a minister.

After the shooting, Noor fled to Ipswich in Suffolk. There he sought refuge with a girlfriend. He turned up at the flat drunk. The two of them watched television together and, when they saw the item about the murder of Michael Dosunmu on the television news, Noor said, 'My boy did the job. The boy was in the bedroom upstairs sleeping, but we didn't want the boy we wanted the brother.'

While naming no names, Noor admitted his part in the murder, though he tried to distance himself from it.

'My boy was terrified and just shot the boy,' he said. 'I was watching in the car outside. I told the boy to go in and do the business.'

After he was arrested, Sannoh, who used the street name Striker, was unrepentant about having killed the wrong person. Interviewed by police he said: 'This boy's brother killed my friend. I don't care about the murder. Fuck the murder. I don't care what happened to that boy.'

Madden stood trial for the murder of Crighton first. Crighton's mother Ivette Brion-Graham said her son had severe sickle-cell anaemia and had met Madden only two weeks before his death. She was not convinced her son was one of the robbers as the only evidence against him were messages sent to his mobile phone.

'In my opinion that is not enough evidence to say he was involved,' she said. 'He never got the chance to defend himself in court. It's very unfair.'

However, Crighton was not on trial. In December 2007, Madden was convicted of his murder and jailed for life with a minimum tariff of 14 years.

At the trial of Sannoh and Noor, the prosecutor Jonathan Laidlaw, QC, told the jury what had led to Michael Dosunmu's tragic death.

'These two men thought it was Hakeem who was sleeping in the bedroom, and he [Michael] was shot because of the money they believed they and their friends had been cheated of – and in revenge for the murder of Javarie Crighton... Michael was just 15. It was he who was asleep in that back bedroom. He had done nothing wrong and nothing of the sort that might make him a target for a shooting of this type.'

Hakeem Dosunmu appeared as a witness and admitted his part in the robberies. Nicknamed 'Soldier', he had gone into crime after a stint in the army, serving with distinction in Bosnia and Iraq. He had already been sentenced to two years imprisonment for armed robbery.

At one point in his testimony he pointed at Sannoh and Noor in the dock and said, 'I know they killed my brother. Ask them why they killed my brother.'

Sannoh's defence barrister Stephen Taylor suggested that Hakeem was a large-scale drug dealer who had amassed a long list of enemies who wanted to kill him. Taylor claimed Hakeem had dealings with many gun-toting gang members in south London, including the Peckham Boys and the Shower Crew, who might have wanted to kill him. He himself had been photographed wielding Mac-10 machine guns. Hakeem replied, 'No, that's what you say. It's all lies.'

Jurors heard Michael and Hakeem's parents were 'hard-working and very respectable' psychiatric nurses. They said they were standing by Hakeem, who was distraught about his brother's death.

'Presently, he is feeling guilty that he brought all this on us,' said Rasak Dosunmu. 'This is not the way we brought him up. He is our son; we love him. We cannot discard him. He made a mistake in life.'

Sannoh and Noor were sentenced to life for Michael Dosunmu's murder and were told they must serve a minimum of 30 years in jail.

Yet another innocent bystander was caught up in the gang war involving the Peckham Boys in late 2007. On 4

October, 26-year-old Polish nurse Magda Pniewska was hit in the head by a stray bullet as two teenage gunmen fired at one another in New Cross. She was talking to her sister in Poland on her mobile phone when she was killed.

A witness, who was too scared to give their name, said the gunmen were aged around 17 or 18 and had quarrelled over an unpaid debt.

'One was leaning into a red Volkswagen Polo and talking to some people,' he said. 'Suddenly the other guy came down the stairs with a bandana covering his face, but you could see his eyes change in a split second, like he thought he was being set up. He pulled out a 9mm handgun from his trousers and fired two or three shots at the car. The other guy got out a similar gun and shot back, using the bonnet for cover. There were about five shots. I don't know where this woman came from – she just came from nowhere. The two guys hit an innocent bystander.'

Another witness said the violence was linked to the local Ghetto Boys gang. He said that, 'Peckham and Wooly Road Youngers are now allied with New Cross and Deptford so the beef can end and lives can be spared.' However, such an alliance between the hood was very disrespectful to the Elders, he said, and the alliance may not hold.

And so the killing went on. Eighteen-year-old student Philip Poru was sitting with a friend in a silver Ford Fiesta in Long Walk car park in Plumstead at around 9.45pm on 14 October 2007 when they were approached by two men who demanded to know what they were doing and where they were from. They made the mistake of saying they were from Peckham. It was the wrong answer. One of the men pulled out a handgun and fired between three and five shots.

Thirty-seven-year-old Gabriel Komolafe came running when he heard the shot and found the two teenagers slumped half out of the car, bleeding heavily. They said they had been shot by a Somalian gang. Komolafe tried to stop blood pouring from Poru's neck before the ambulance came. It did no good. Poru died. His 18-year-old friend was also seriously injured and was kept under armed guard in hospital.

'We were parking when we found them,' said Komolafe. 'My hands were covered in blood and I'd left my two little boys and partner in the car – it was horrible.'

The inquest concluded that the shooting had been carried out by members of a gang known as the Woolwich Somalians. Poru and his friend had walked into a gang war. Two weeks before, two Woolwich gang members had been shot and injured by the T-Block gang from Thamesmead who were predominately Nigerian. T-Block were said to be allied with the Peckham Boys, who also had a large number of Nigerian members. So when the two students said they were from Peckham, it was assumed that they had come to Woolwich territory on behalf of T-Block. Poru and his friend, who were entirely innocent, had been in the wrong place at the wrong time.

'The Somalians are trying to take over the estate from the other Africans and run all the drugs and guns on it,' said a witness. 'It's a war zone. They're fighting over it street by street. There's kids as young as 11 being dragged into this.'

In the autumn of 2008, the police decided to crack down

on the Peckham Boys. On 23 September, officers from the flying squad made dawn raids on 17 homes across south London. They arrested seven suspected Peckham Boy members, described as major players, connected to over 120 violent robberies in 17 different London boroughs, netting some £200,000 over the previous 17 months. Members were believed to have been targeting gaming machines, betting shops, arcades and pubs, threatening their victims with knives, machetes, crowbars and screwdrivers up to 18 inches in length. During the raid two Samurai swords were recovered.

CHAPTER 2

TAMIL SNAKE GANG

In the 1990s, gun crime began to spread within the Tamil, Sikh, Indian, Pakistani and Bengali communities, and the murder rate tripled over the decade up to 2003. There were more than 40 murders involving South Asians and 228 kidnappings in that year alone.

In 2003 Scotland Yard created a specialist squad – the Tamil Taskforce – to deal solely with the rising gangland violence in the Sri Lankan Tamil communities following 13 gang-related murders centred among Tamils in Ilford, Walthamstow, Newham and Wembley. Tamil gangs also controlled drug trafficking and prostitution in the area. The same situation existed in Toronto, Canada, where large numbers of expatriate Tamils live.

The rise in violence among the Tamil communities first raised serious concern in the late 1990s following a spate of stabbings and street fights between rival groups across London. The first Tamil murder to be given media attention was in 2002 when a charred body was found in Roe Green Park, Kingsbury, north-west London. It belonged to 18-year-old Sri Lankan student Supenthar Ramachandran, who was studying maths and science at Harrow College. He had come from Sri Lanka to study in England with the aim of lifting his family out of poverty. He got to know 22-year-old Senthamil Thillainathan – known simply as 'Tamil' – and his accomplices Pradeep Sivaneesan and Satheeskumar Arulanathan, both 18, and 30-year-old Kannan Sivakumar. Ramachandran sought their protection from Muslims who were bullying him at college.

The gang took Ramachandran to the Palm Beach restaurant in Ealing Road, Wembley. After they had eaten, they demanded £200 from Ramachandran to pay the bill. Then they drove their terrified victim to Roe Green Park in Kingsbury, where he was savagely beaten, stripped naked, doused with petrol and set on fire. Ramachandran's charred remains were found the following day by a horrified passer-by.

Thillainathan, Sivaneesan, Arulanathan and Sivakumar were arrested and charged with murder. At their trial, prosecutor Aftab Jafferjee said that Ramachandran was a frail youth who had been slaughtered like a frightened animal. He told the jury not to look for any logic or sense in why Ramachandran had been killed, but simply to accept the murder as 'sheer cruelty'.

Thillainathan, who had an address in Kingswinford on the outskirts of Birmingham as well as one in Wembley, was also charged with the murder of 25-year-old Arvithan Muthukamarasamy eight months before the death of

Ramachandran. Thillainathan and a car-load of friends blamed Muthukamarasamy for scratching a BMW that belonged to one of the killers. Muthukamarasamy and four friends had spent the day in Wembley watching and playing cricket. They went to a music store before returning to their car at 9.30pm. There Muthukamarasamy was attacked. One of the assailants stabbed him in the hand, leaving part of it hanging off. The victim recognised one of the people who was attacking him and said, 'Why are you doing this?' The attacker's response was to strike him in the head with an axe, slicing off the top of his scalp.

'He had axe wounds to his head, shattering his skull,' said Jafferjee. 'He had seven stab wounds to his torso and one of them went fifteen centimetres into his lung.'

Thillainathan had also attacked four other men in the car with Muthukamarasamy, leaving two permanently scarred.

Muthukamarasamy was not even responsible for the damage to the BMW. The gang had made a 'ghastly misidentification,' Jafferjee said. 'Even if there was substance to what they believed, these men embarked upon what was an act of revenge of almost unimaginable ferocity.'

Thillainathan denied murdering both Muthukamarasamy in June 2001 and Ramachandran in February 2002 but was convicted of murder and four counts of wounding with intent. He was given two life sentences with four terms of ten years, to run concurrently. The previous October 23-year-old Sivageethan Punniyamoorthy of Northolt, north London, was also convicted of murdering Muthukamarasamy, and given a life sentence. At that time, the jury couldn't agree on a verdict in Thillainathan's case, so he was retried for that offence at the same time as the Kingsbury murder.

Thillainathan's accomplices – Sivaneesan, Arulanathan and Sivakumar – also denied murdering Ramachandran. All three were convicted. Sivaneesan and Arulanathan were ordered to be detained during Her Majesty's pleasure. Sivakumar was jailed for life. In mitigation, the court heard that Sivakumar had been a Tamil Tiger during the civil war in Sri Lanka. He later escaped to Britain, where he sought asylum.

The case against Thillainathan, Sivaneesan, Arulanathan and Sivakumar at the Old Bailey had originally been scheduled for eight weeks. It took seven months and cost £17 million.

Two months after Ramachandran was found dead in Kingsbury, a 19-year-old Sri Lankan suffered serious head wounds after being repeatedly struck with a weapon as he parked in Croydon. There was a Tamil-on-Tamil killing in Merton, then three Tamils were charged with attempted murder. And in November 2001, 36-year-old laundry manager Sellathurai Balasingham was attacked by six men near a grassy area in Mitcham, south-west London. He was taken by ambulance to the Mayday Hospital in Croydon where he was declared dead shortly after midnight on 7 November. In July 2008, 26-year-old Prabu Santharatnam and 29-year-old Nimalan Nadarajah were convicted of his murder and perverting the course of justice. Thirty-three-year-old Jathies Santharatnam and 28-year-old Mayuran Seevaratnam were convicted of manslaughter. Santharatnam was also convicted of perverting the course of justice. The other two – 28-year-old Nimalrajah Thambithurai and 29-year-old Makundan Kumarasritharan – were found guilty of conspiracy to assault.

It became clear that gang warfare was breaking out when 26-year-old Suresh Kumar Selvarajah was shot at point-blank range. He was killed in his home in Lyon Park Avenue, Wembley when one of the killers had been trying to execute his father-in-law.

Neighbours said they heard two shots from the semi-detached house. Afterwards two Asian men were seen fleeing. Medics could not save the victim, who was pronounced dead at the scene.

The murder was blamed on the Tamil Snake Gang who, hours before, had attempted to kill Paramalingham in a drive-by shooting. In November 2003, Ragulaperuman Sachchithananthan, 27, and Nagarisa Sivakumar, 33, were jailed for life for the cold-blooded killing of Selvarajah.

It seems that rivalry had broken out between Tamil gangs in Wembley and Ilford. This resulted in tit-for-tat murders. On the warm Saturday night of 7 June 2003, Partheepan Balasingham was drinking with friends outside the popular Sri Lankan Palm Beach restaurant in north-west London, the same restaurant student Supenthar Ramachandran had been in before he was killed. Balasingham was taking a rare break between his two jobs as a factory packer and bakery worker. The pavement meeting-point was popular with young Tamils in the area; Sri Lankans often played all-night cricket in the car park nearby. According to his passport, 23-year-old Balasingham was supposed to be a student. He was living with his 15-year-old brother in London, but there was no record of him attending college. However, he had not been in trouble with the police.

At 1am, a car pulled up in Ealing Road. Five men got out

and rushed towards Balasingham. They hacked him around the head and neck with a machete, a sword and bottles. The force of the blows fractured his skull and he died from his injuries in hospital five days later. His assailants fled the scene and sped off eastwards.

An hour later, at around 2am on Sunday, about a dozen young Tamils confronted six others outside the Icon Bar in Ilford, east London. A fight broke out and two of the six were bundled into two cars. One of those abducted was 18-year-old student Kishokumar Balachandiran, who lived with his mother and three young sisters in rented rooms in Stanmore, north-west London. He was found ten hours later by a dog walker, sitting in the Roding river in nearby Wanstead, semi-conscious and in shock. He had wounds on his face, neck, shoulder and stomach, and was suffering from hypothermia. The police said he had been beaten and possibly tortured for several hours. He died of his injuries six days later. The other abductee, Jaydee Rumapathy, who had been bundled into a green Rover, was punched in the face but survived.

Postmortem examinations found that the cut-marks on the back of the two murder victims' heads were very similar and were probably inflicted with a similar weapon – a machete, sword or meat cleaver. The police believed that the attack on Balachandiran was a case of mistaken identity. Later that month, the police raided addresses in Barkingside and Ilford, arresting 15 young men in their late teens and early twenties.

On the afternoon of Saturday, 27 September 2003, 18-year-old Asan Ratnasargan was sitting in a red Alfa Romeo coupé with two friends at the traffic lights marking the junction of Ealing Road and Carlyon Road in Wembley. A red saloon that had been following them stopped behind. Four men got out brandishing samurai swords. They attacked the car with the hammers and axes, before stabbing Asan in the chest with the sword and killing him. His two terrified friends drove off to escape, but it was too late. The killers also fled the scene.

Asan had been born in Sri Lanka. He had been living with relatives in London for two years and worked in the family's shops. He had no known link to crime and police could not understand why he was picked out. They thought that the Tamil Ari Ala Gang was responsible for his murder. However, many gang names identified by police were simply the names of Sri Lankan settlements where the individuals involved came from, and it is thought the gang names were given to these groups by the police rather than by the gangs themselves.

Chief Inspector Derrick Griffiths of the Tamil Taskforce says there are five main Tamil gangs in London. They are based in East Ham and Walthamstow in east London, Wembley in north-west London and Merton and Croydon in south London. The East Ham group is the biggest with 30 core members. It is believed that they use the M25 or the North Circular – sometimes driving in convoy – to launch attacks between Ilford and Wembley.

Tamil gangs finance their activities by credit-card fraud. In July 2003, the police smashed a highly organised £6-million credit-card scam. Operating from fried-chicken restaurants in north-west London, the fraudsters set up factories to 'clone' or reproduce scores of fake credit cards.

Used the fake cards, they had access to 98 different accounts and stole £6.35 million in four months. In some cases, the swindlers even handed in fake credit cards to banks to claim the £50 reward for each lost or stolen card returned. The police seized at least a hundred fake cards, some disguised as supermarket loyalty cards to avoid detection. The raids were carried out by officers from the Dedicated Cheque and Plastic Crime Unit, set up to combat the multimillion pound trade in credit-card fraud.

On the trail of Sri Lankan murderers, some 500 officers searched homes in Newham, Waltham Forest, Redbridge, Harrow, Brent and Croydon. They arrested 13 suspects and seized a pistol, ammunition, swords, axes, baseball bats and pickaxe handles. In Newham, more credit-card cloning equipment was found. The police seized 69 credit cards, £11,000 in cash, blank cheques worth up to £4,500 and a £30,000 Mercedes in Waltham Forest.

Another fraud that had been running, the police feared, from 2002 was ended in 2007. Called the 'London Conspiracy', a six-man gang, which included two illegal immigrants, used cloned credit cards and cheques that would later bounce to obtain cash-back from supermarkets and to buy cigarettes and alcohol, which were then sold on to fellow Tamils running off-licences. They also bought chips at six London casinos, used a few and redeemed the remainder for cash. The six were given jail terms of between two years, nine months and five years. The two illegal immigrants were recommended for deportation at the end of their sentences.

Meanwhile the Tamil Tigers got into the action, installing machinery to 'skim' data from credit and debit cards at some two hundred petrol stations in London, Hull, Leeds, Liverpool, Edinburgh, Norfolk, Peterborough, Bristol and Nottingham. The information was then transferred to bogus cards and used to obtain funds in Thailand, which were then used to support the Tamil Tigers' military campaign in Sri Lanka. Millions of pounds were taken. In all, the police reckon that Tamil gangs were making over £35 million a year in credit-card fraud. They also earned money by extortion. In Newham, for instance, gang members demand £10,000 to £15,000 a year from shops and businesses, and also confiscate cars from people and demand up to £3,000 for their return.

South of the river, Tamil Snake Gang member Sugandthan Nadarajah, also known as 'Sugu', worked as an 'enforcer' or a 'soldier' for other affiliated gangs. He was directly involved in a variety of co-ordinated attacks against other gangs in the region – before he earned the nickname 'The Mad Axe Man' in Croydon's 'London Road Street Murder'.

Back in 2001, 24-year-old Nadarajah had been involved in an incident in Croydon. While being chased by a rival gang, he was hit by a car and run over, ending up in intensive care with bad shoulder and leg injuries. When he got out of hospital, he was determined to get even and on the night of 28 October 2003 he was out looking for revenge. He was with 31-year-old Shanthan Tharamalingam, 22-year-old Sasikaran Selveratnam and 26-year-old Ranjan Shanmughanathan. They were part of a four-man team that worked as a sister group to the Tamil Strike Team, who made regular incursions and attacks in Croydon.

That night, 28-year-old Thirukar Sothilingam, a fellow

Tamil, and a friend went to the Flaming Grill kebab house in London Road, West Croydon. The gang found Sothilingam's Vauxhall Corsa parked nearby and began to smash it up, believing it was the car involved in the crash that had injured Nadarajah. And when Thirukar Sothilingam returned to his car he was felled by four axe blows and left in a pool of blood. He died 12 hours later in Charing Cross Hospital.

After the attack the killers ran off towards Croydon town centre and one witness told police it was as if they were celebrating a victory. They had weapons in their hands and, as they ran away, they were waving them and shouting in triumph. Half an hour later they were arrested. Nadarajah was found with cuts on his right hand. His blood was found on the axe and his trainers were stained with a mixture of his own and the victim's blood. Glass was found on three of the men's clothing.

At the Old Bailey, Nadarajah and Tharamalingam blamed each other for the murder, while Selveratnam and Shanmughanathan refused to give evidence. This did not matter, said Sir Allan Green, QC, prosecuting. They plainly had a common cause. Earlier in the evening they had held a 'council of war'.

'The axeman, we say, is clearly guilty of murder because he very brutally and savagely dealt that man at least four heavy blows that ultimately killed him,' he said. 'This was part of a joint enterprise and the others were in it with him, and they were not only interested in damaging the car but anyone who came to the car as the unfortunate victim did.'

The prosecution claimed Nadarajah had delivered the fatal blows, but the jury was unable to decide who was the axeman. Nevertheless, all four were found guilty of murder. Nadarajah and Tharamalingam were also found guilty of criminal damage, a charge that Selveratnam and Shanmughanathan had admitted earlier. Judge Anthony Morris sentenced all four men to life imprisonment and ordered that they each serve a minimum of 14 years.

'This was a planned offence,' said Judge Morris. 'It also involved the carrying and intention to use the axe as a weapon against the person. None of you have been found to be the axeman so you are all sentenced as secondary parties.'

Meanwhile, Sri Lankan gangs from east and west London continued their deadly rivalry. On 28 August 2006, 23-year-old Arulmurugan Sebamalai and other members of the DMX Tamil gang were going to play cricket when they were set upon by the East Ham Boys, led by 21-year-old Senthurrajah Thavapalasingham, also known as 'Psycho'. They were carrying knives, baseball bats, swords and pickaxe handles studded with bolts.

Some 25 gang members had driven over from Newham to Wembley in five cars. It seems they were looking for Sebamalai. They tracked him to Braemar Avenue in Brent. When they spotted him in a white Suzuki Swift with his friends, witnesses said they surrounded it and started throwing bottles at the car. Alarmed by the attack Ashokumar Tharmarajah, who was driving the car, stopped and the group got out, arming themselves with cricket bats and stumps. Thavapalasingham and fellow gang member 32-year-old Kirubananantharasa Gunaratnam, known as 'Kiruba', got out of their green BMW and took two swords out of the boot.

'Psycho was armed with a samurai sword,' Sebamalai told the police. 'The sword was around three feet long, silver coloured. It wasn't in a sheath. He was holding it in a raised position and running towards us. I got out of the car and I had a bat in my hand. When he started cutting me repeatedly I tried to block it.'

Armed with swords and pickaxe handles, the East Ham Boys singled out Sebamalai and rained down a series of blows as gang members shouted, 'Slash him, Psycho, kill him.'

Sebamalai was struck on the head by a bottle, and when he fell to the ground both Thavapalasingham and Gunaratnam attacked him with their swords, trying to behead him. Sebamalai lifted his cricket bat in an attempt to shield his head – but the razor-sharp sword sliced through his left forearm, exposing the bone and partially severing his arm. There was little the victim's friends, Tharmarajah and Lynkaran Tharmalingam, could do was they watched Sebamalai being slashed. The fight was eventually broken up by police.

Thavapalasingham was arrested at the scene while Gunaratnam was arrested hiding in a nearby street. They were caught with the bloodstained samurai sword. Sebamalai had identified Thavapalasingham and Gunaratnam as his attackers at an identification parade. Thavapalasingham and Gunaratnam were convicted of attempted murder and violent disorder at the Old Bailey after a three-month trial in 2008. Thavapalasingham also confessed that he was going to offer the victim's family £40,000 if Sebamalai did not pick him out in the identity parade.

The judge, Richard Hawkings, QC, said it was a pre-planned attack with dangerous weapons designed to inflict grave injuries on their victim.

'You were armed with a samurai sword and other weapons, and had come specifically prepared to cause violence,' he said. 'I am referring to a stick with bolts protruding from it. In full view, you attempted to kill.'

He sentenced Thavapalasingham and Gunaratnam to life imprisonment with a minimum tariff of 12 years. The seven members of Thavapalasingham's gang were sentenced to a total of 63 years. Interestingly, their arrests saw an enormous 80 per cent drop in criminal damage in the London borough of Newham. Antisocial behaviour fell by half and extortion from local shop owners virtually halted. A series of crackdowns, patrols and the installation of CCTV cameras on the High Street drove the remaining criminals into hiding.

Things were getting too hot for some gang members. In February 2007, a 26-year-old Tamil from east London, who would give his name only as Abhya, announced that he was giving up gang life. His involvement had left him with a circular scar that almost encircled his right eye.

'That was someone trying to take my eye out with a broken beer bottle,' he said. Then he pointed to his forehead. 'And this here was a cut from a samurai sword.'

The cut extended from his hairline to his right eyebrow. It was the result of an altercation with a rival gang at a wedding in 2005 in Ilford.

'They chased me down the High Street,' he said. 'When I confronted them, one of them cut me on the forehead.'

It was the death of a 23-year-old friend that persuaded him to change his ways.

'He was watching TV downstairs and I was upstairs with other guys when a group wearing masks came and shot him three times through the window,' said Abhya. 'He died on my birthday.'

Of the ten murders among London's 100,000-strong Tamil community that occurred between 2000 and 2007, only two cases had been successfully brought to court.

'All the crimes were detected and people were charged,' said Chief Inspector Derrick Griffiths of the Tamil Taskforce, 'but what we found was the level of intimidation was so high that we couldn't get anybody from the Tamil community to come to court and give evidence.'

Coercion is real problem. Fifty-eight-year-old Vellupillai Jegendira Bose, who owns an estate agency on East Ham High Street, faced the wrath of the gangs when he attended a community meeting called by the police.

'After the meeting I was joking with the officer that I may need protection,' he said. 'When I returned, someone had shattered the display window of the shop.'

Most of the violence has resulted from inter-gang rivalries and revenge attacks stemming from territorial control, community leaders believe.

And while Adhya may have given up gang life, there are plenty more recruits to replace him.

'Boys of 12 and 14 are being lured by the gangs,' said Mala Krishnaraja, head of the Tamil Community Forum. 'The attraction of having money and flashy cars and the show of power gets the children interested in gang culture.'

The police carry out regular raids to seize weapons from gang hideouts. While their weapons of choice seem to be samurai swords, axes and daggers, some of the leadership now carry pistols.

According to the police, Sri Lankan gangs in south London are constantly 'tooled up'. In June 2007, 28-year-old Prabaskaran Kannan was chased through Tooting by four men from Croydon who stabbed and slashed their terrified victim 31 times outside a fried chicken takeaway. Witnesses said that Kannan was heard shouting, 'It wasn't me, it wasn't me,' shortly before he was brutally set upon and killed in what became known as the 'Chicken Cottage murder'. Two men with him suffered lesser injuries.

The Jaffna Boys had been engaged in a long-running gang war with the victim's Tooting Tamils gang, which resulted in the police being called to at least 80 separate incidents. On the night of Mr Kannan's murder, members of the two gangs had exchanged insults and been involved in a series of street clashes.

The four members of the Jaffna Boys wept as they were convicted of Kannan's murder at the Old Bailey. Judge Martin Stephens, QC, described the murder as 'an attack of exceptional ferocity'. Aziz Miah and Asif Kumbay, both 20, and Vabeesan Shivarajah, 22, were each ordered to serve at least 17 years, while 18-year-old Kirush Nanthankumar must serve at least 14 years. Kumbay, Shivarajah and Miah were also given jail sentences for attacking two of Mr Kannan's friends, which will run concurrently to their life terms.

Two other members of the Croydon gang were cleared of murder and manslaughter but convicted of assault. Their conviction came as a relief to one businessman who runs a shop in Croydon. He said that Sri Lankan Tamil gangs controlled most of the crime and had the town centre on 'lockdown'.

Sri Lankan gangs are seeemingly fearless and are not afraid of committing their crimes in daylight, in front of witnesses. In April 2008, two Sri Lankans were dragged out of a van in Tooting, south-west London, and beaten to death in the street by a gang of up to 20 men armed with iron bars, poles and even house 'For Sale' signs. A third man in the van escaped.

'It just looked like two groups having a bit of a ruckus,' said an eyewitness. 'Then I saw a youth lying on the ground with five men beating him over and over again. It was like a scene on a TV crime series, not a quiet street in Tooting – then I realised it was gang warfare being played out right in front of me.'

Another witness saw passers-by running away in terror.

A resident said, 'I'd heard that trouble had been simmering between Tamil and Sri Lankan gangs for weeks.'

CHAPTER 3

THE GOOCHES AND THE DODDINGTONS

Manchester's Gooch Close Gang sprang up in the early 1980s. They took their name from Gooch Close, a road in Moss Side that now no longer exists. Their money came from the supply of heroin, which was taking over as the recreational drug of choice at that time. They soon gained a reputation for violence when they started a turf war with the rival Cheetham Hill Gang for control of the city centre.

In the 1960s, as Moss Side expanded, a spill-over estate was built north of the city at Cheetham Hill and many of Moss Side's Afro-Caribbeans decamped to the area, which is smaller and more compact than the sprawling council estates of Hulme and Moss Side. Some drug dealing went on, mainly in the pubs, but this was nothing like the multimillion pound business carried on in Moss Side. Because it is smaller, however, its criminal community was more tightly knit. They were tougher and, consequently, more dangerous.

The gang from Cheetham Hill were also in conflict with a gang from the Alexandra Park estate who were dealing from Moss Lane. They became known as the Pepperhill Mob. The Cheetham Hill Gang moved in on them, provoking a gang war. There had already been eight shootings and one drug-related murder when the deputy head of Greater Manchester CID warned: 'We are dealing with a black mafia which is a threat to the whole community, and fear that unless we can apprehend the leaders, it is only a matter of time before an innocent person is killed. Only last Tuesday a shotgun was blasted at the bedroom window of a house where a woman and child live. On Wednesday a man was shot in the foot.'

The shootings began in the spring of 1987 with the murder of 49-year-old Ivan Preston, a doorman at a Moss Side shebeen. Two months later there was a second shooting when Anthony 'Soldier' Baker blasted teenager Julian Bradshaw at close range. Bradshaw had been armed with a machete or nightstick. Baker shot him as he lay wounded and defenceless on the floor pleading for his life. Baker was sentenced life imprisonment, to serve a minimum of 20 years.

Petty criminal Tony Gardener was killed when his car pulled up outside an illegal drinking den in January 1988. It seemed he had been set up, although his killing may well have been a case of mistaken identity. Then, in June 1990, Hendey Proverbs was shot for no apparent reason while drinking in the Spinners, a pub on the fringes of Moss Side which, at the time, had seen better days. Superintendent Ronald Gaffey recalled the scene. 'As I walked in the barman looks up at me, still pulling his pint, and jerks his head in the direction of a body lying on the floor in a pool of blood. At a nearby table two men were casually finishing off their pints. In the room next door a game of pool was still going on. A man had been murdered at close range with a shotgun. It was an awful mess, blood dripping off the walls. And yet, judging by their reactions, you'd think nothing had happened. This isn't Washington. This is Manchester. Things like that aren't supposed to happen here.'

The murders quickly mounted. Between March and June 1990 sixteen guns were confiscated by the police. Local gangsters were carrying a range of weaponry, from James Bond-style Walther PPK 8mm handguns, .38 Smith & Wessons and Colt .45s to sawn-off shotguns and Uzi sub-machine guns. There had been 30 documented shoots so far that year and the police estimated there were another hundred that had gone unreported. The wounded even discharged themselves from hospital to stay away from the police. More people, who had connections to Manchester, were shot in Leeds.

The Cheetham Hill Gang branched out into armed robbery. In 1990, two of them were imprisoned for 42 years for attempted murder and the robbery of a Securicor van. The driver was shot at point-blank range trying to crawl to safety under the van and had to have his leg amputated.

They also tried to move in on Manchester's clubland, barging their way into clubs and demanding free drinks. The police refused to take them on and so the club owners had to eject them using pickaxe handles as weapons.

What no one could ignore was that kids were getting involved with the gangs from an early age. Even before they were in their teens they were running messages, seduced by easy money. It would begin with a dealer giving them £5 to buy patties for his lunch. When the kid came back with £2 change, the dealer would tell him to keep it. Pretty soon, the kid would be finding new customers for the dealer's drugs – and taking a commission. Then he would become a scout, watching out for the police for street dealers. After that, he would start selling the stuff himself. In April 1990, a 16-year-old boy was found with £30 wraps of heroin and a safe deposit box with £5,000 of cash in it. School could not compete. No kid was going to work hard to pass his exams if he was already earning more than his teachers. The parents weren't a problem either. When a lad gave his mother £500 to take a holiday back home in Jamaica, few asked where the money came from.

By 1990, there were estimated to be 300 dealers making up to £1,000 a day in Moss Side alone. They had a turnover of well over £20 million a year. Their presence on the street had scared off shoppers. Legitimate businesses closed. The only shop in the area that remained open was a sports' store selling Ellesse trainers at £70 a pair. The dealers all wore expensive trainers, shell-suits, gold watches and bracelets; they drove BMWs and Mercedes – all bought for cash. Few risked opening a bank account, preferring to keep their money under the bed at home.

However, this ostentation left dealers vulnerable to 'taxing'. The poorer dealers could easily see who was making the money. They would wait until a rich dealer came home then burst in wearing masks and carrying guns. Those caught this way had no choice but to hand over their cash. One dealer lost £60,000 this way – and there was no one he could report it to. Soon dealers were ditching the gold bracelets, watches and BMWs. Some drug gangsters took to wearing combat fatigues with military flak jackets for protection. The bulletproof equipment was not just for show or bravado; shoot-outs between the rival gangs became a daily occurrence.

The local MP, Tony Lloyd, commiserated with Moss Side's suffering – and the suffering of the 95 per cent of law-abiding citizens there. He could also understand the reluctance of the police to crack down, as it would only push the problem into neighbouring constituencies. There was even a suspicion that the police would prefer to contain the problem in a predominantly 'black' area, rather than risk exporting it to a middle-class white area where the residents would soon be up in arms.

'If there were jobs it wouldn't be so bad,' said Lloyd. 'I guess you could say the dealers are just part of the enterprise culture.'

However, there were deeper fears.

'My main worry is that if the 1981 riots were to flare up again,' he said, 'this time the black kids would not be throwing bottles and stones; they'd be shooting off guns.'

In May 1990, there was a confrontation at the Bob Marley memorial concert in Moss Side's Alexandra Park. It was just a blatant show of strength. Gang members poured out of cars and lined up. It was a hot day, but the gangsters were wearing mackintoshes or padded coats, hiding the guns they were carrying.

'They just came straight into the park and started to walk across, chanting, towards the crowd,' said one drug dealer. At it was, nothing happened. But it put the fear of God into those who attended. In the world of drug dealing, reputation is power.

It was in this atmosphere that the Gooch Gang came of age. By the summer of 1990, half a dozen lads – some in their teens, most in their early twenties – could be seen standing around the quiet cul-de-sac waiting for trade. Some carried mobile phones; others straddled mountain bikes. Both were essential tools. In those days, a cellphone was difficult to tap and the dealer could move about undetected. The customer could call in an order, then runners as young as 12 on mountain bikes that cost up to £500 would be despatched to pick up the drugs from a nearby hiding place and deliver them. If the police approached, they could make a quick getaway down the back alleys and over the grass verges, making it hard to follow them. And, when it came to guns, the Gooch Close lads already had a fearsome reputation.

As the Manchester dance scene faltered in the early 1990s, the dealers who had sold ecstasy and other designer drugs to the rave market were forced out of the centre of town to compete with the heroin dealers in Moss Side. Mayhem ensued.

There were random drive-by shootings. In March 1991, six shots were fired at 14-year-old schoolboy Paul Sahedo and 12-year-old Anthony Richards. Paul was hit in the hip. Anthony lost his left eye. Neither had anything to do with drugs. Nevertheless, a wave of reprisals followed. A gang dragged a 20-year-old man from a pub and hacked him with a machete. There were at least two other assaults with machetes around that time.

Later that year, 27-year-old drug dealer Richard Bowen came up from Birmingham to a house in Rosebery Street near Alexandra Park in Moss Side to buy heroin. He was blasted in the face with a shotgun. It is thought that he never even got to meet a dealer – they rarely shoot buyers as it makes people wary of the trade. Rather, it is thought he met an addict who killed him for the £100 he had in his pocket.

That weekend, two other men were shot in Moss Side. One was hit in the leg as a masked man ran out of the Pepperhill pub in Bedwell Close firing a pistol at a group of youths. A stray bullet smashed through the dining-room window of the house of a mother and her four children, all of whom were in the house at the time. A few hundred yards away, a man was shot in the arm. Nearby, in the fading Victorian inner-city enclave of Whalley Range, a 23-year-old was attacked by a group of youths, one of them wielding a machete. Meanwhile, the council were meeting with the police, discussing how to protect their workers. Two had been beaten up in Moss Side after being seen using mobile phones; local gangsters had assumed they were undercover cops.

By this time it was clear that there were two factions on the Alexandra Park estate involved in a turf war – the Pepperhill Mob, the other from Gooch Close. They lived just a quarter-of-a-mile apart on an estate that had only 3,000 residents.

It was thought, briefly, that the Cheetham Hill Gang was trying to move in. On 8 March, their leader Tony Hill was killed. By then, guns were everywhere. You could get one for £50 in a matter of hours. Fifty were seized by the police in 18 months. A man who moved up to Moss Side from south London said, 'There probably were guns in Brixton, but you never saw them. Here we have had two shootings at either end of our street. You walk down the road and run into gangs of kids selling drugs. It's time to leave.'

Less than a month after Richard Bowen was killed, 19-year-old Winston Brownlow was shot in the hand by a motorcyclist who kept his visor down. Five hours later, 17-year-old Carl Stapleton was hacked to death a couple of hundred yards from the base of the Gooch Close Gang. A member of the Pepperhill gang told the *Observer* newspaper: 'We have the guns and knives to hit back at the Gooch Close gang and we can do it, I promise you.'

Soon after the police raided the Pepperhill pub, keeping a helicopter hovering outside. But the man they were looking for was not there. An hour later, a phalanx of youths turned up, entering the pub in a wedge formation. They, too, came away empty handed. Soon there were burning cars in the street.

The gang war sparked other horrific reprisals. The body of a 67-year-old man was found in Moss Side wrapped in a plastic sheet. His body was pierced with dozens of stab wounds. The remains of a young black man were found in an abandoned flat. He had been locked in a wardrobe with two pit bull terriers. In a derelict house, rooms were found covered in blood, with no further clues as to who had died there. The newspapers began describing Manchester as 'Gangchester' or 'Gunchester' and 'The Bronx of Britain'. Things got so bad that the Manchester Police sought advice from their counterparts in Miami.

In August 1991, as part of Operation China, undercover

policemen were used to buy drugs and over 300 transactions involving heroin were filmed using hidden cameras. The police raided a dozen homes in the area, seizing shotguns, handguns, knives, machetes and a crossbow. Twenty gang members, one as young as fifteen, were sentenced to a total of 109 years' imprisonment.

But this did not stop the gunfire. In the first ten months of 1992, there were six murders in the area and there were a hundred reported shootings in just four months. The police reported that increasingly young gangsters were settling their disputes with guns. In just ten days in November, there were at least four shoot-outs in the street – all within half-a-mile of the Moss Side divisional police station. On 25 November, a young man sprayed a shopping precinct with a semi-automatic pistol in an attempt to eliminate a rival. The bullets sent scores of afternoon shoppers, many of them with young children, diving for cover. The incident was barely reported in the national newspapers. No arrests were made and the teenage gunman simply disappeared in the confusion.

The following day, a man was forced into his own car at gunpoint by four youths wearing balaclavas and bandanas and driven to a derelict house in Moss Side where they tried to extort £30,000 from him. He escaped by jumping through a plate-glass window. A gang of youths broke into a community centre where a social evening for elderly people was being held. They made the guests hand over their money and valuables. Nobody resisted. Nevertheless, without saying a word, one of the gang walked over to a 75-year-old lady and smashed a baseball bat against her legs as she sat in a chair.

It was known that one Moss Side drugs baron enjoyed terrorising elderly women. He carried a handgun openly in the street and was known simply as 'Evil'. Just 16, he already had a harem of three young women he called 'The Bitches'. He controlled an army of schoolboy couriers who delivered drugs on expensive mountain bikes. They wore a uniform – baseball jackets and caps with brightly coloured bandanas hiding their faces.

Another notorious dealer at the time was Delroy, who had been shot several times in the back. They said he had more lives than a cat. If you saw him at a bus stop, the saying went, take a cab. Such gang leaders held absolute sway. In one incident three families were told at 3pm to be out of Moss Side that day. By 8pm, all of them had taken their children and gone, leaving behind most of their belongings. They had left so hastily that their television sets were still turned on.

On 2 January 1993, 14-year-old Benji Stanley was caught in crossfire as he queued for a takeaway outside Alvino's Pattie and Dumplin' shop in Moss Side. He was blasted at close range by a single-barrelled pump-action shotgun, just a hundred yards from his home. The killer was wearing a combat jacket and a balaclava. He ran to a silver-coloured car. As he opened the door to make his getaway, music blasted out. Five days earlier, the grocers shop next door had been robbed by three men with shotguns and sledgehammers.

'They took £200 and our best champagne,' said shopkeeper Zulfikar Nazir. 'I'd like to leave, but I'm not a rich guy who can say, "Bugger this" and shut up shop. I'll have to stay till I'm dead.'

Others did sell up, making a substantial loss on their property. Fifteen years later Manchester's Cold Case Review Unit was still looking into the murder of Benji Stanley.

According to the head of the Greater Manchester drugs squad, the gangsters used guns to enhance their status.

'They love walking around with a gun on them,' said Detective Superintendent David Brennan. 'They revel in the "respect" that goes with having money, access to drugs, and a gun ... For them, violence works; the more extreme the violence, the more status it brings.'

The Pepperhill Gang moved their drug operations to nearby Doddington Close. Now the battle lines were drawn between the 'Goochies' and the 'Doddies', who controlled the west side and east side of Alexandra Park respectively. The Goochies wore red bandanas; the Doddies blue. Both gangs used children with mountain bikes as couriers to deliver heroin, crack and 'ice' – an amphetamine-based version of crack. Among gangsters, being a 'ride' became a euphemism for gang membership.

All of the big dealers in Moss Side – and there were 40 to 50 of them – owned or had access to weapons. For £50 you could buy a handgun; £300 would get you a sub-machine gun. Gangsters were carrying Sten guns and AK-47s. They came from legitimate retailers who had gone 'over the wall', or they were stolen, or brought into the country in containers – an easy route given the reduction in European border controls.

In the Moss Side Leisure and Shopping Centre, the locals were terrorised into turning a blind eye by delinquents who stared unblinkingly at strangers and made a curiously menacing clicking sound with the tongue against the roof of their mouths. The police were powerless. Radio scanners detected their imminent arrival. Gangsters would simply disappear into a warren of rat-runs and the police would find themselves at war with an unseen enemy.

Just four months after Benji Stanley was shot and killed, 19-year-old GCSE college student Andrea Mairs heard screeching tyres and gunshots from the street below. She pulled back her bedroom curtains to see what was happening. As she and her mother, Eula, peered through the dark at a gang of youths on a nearby corner, they were silhouetted in the window of their first-floor flat beside Manchester's notorious Moss Side tower blocks. Andrea said she saw up to half a dozen figures in the street. One of them was carrying an automatic rifle or machine gun. Then she felt a sharp pain in her chest and cried to her mother, 'Mum, I've been hit.'

Across the street a taxi driver, Mohammed Bhamjee, his wife Maymuma and their five children, escaped injury when a bullet smashed through their front door. In nearby Norton Street another bullet narrowly missed an old lady, and an elderly couple cowered beneath the bed after their bedroom window was smashed. Two other homes were hit by indiscriminate fire.

The bullet that hit Andrea passed straight through her body. It missed her heart by less than an inch but bruised her lung before lodging in the bedroom wall. Fortunately her mother was an auxiliary nurse and could administer first aid. After emergency surgery at Manchester Royal Infirmary, Andrea recovered. But when she returned home, she was too terrified to venture out. She was unfit to sit her GCSEs and had to undergo psychological counselling.

'Sometimes she will slip into another world,' said her mother, 'and I don't have to guess what she is thinking. She was in no fit state to do her exams.'

In early July 1993, three men burst into The Sports pub in Whalley Range at closing time. They were wearing combat fatigues, their faces covered with bandanas, and they were carrying two automatic pistols and a sub-machine gun. They stood on seats and fired an estimated 30 rounds at a group of around 40 people sitting on a raised platform in the crowded lounge. The machine gunner seemed to lose control of his weapon in the rapid firing. Bullets smacked into the walls. A 22-year-old man, who had been acquitted of the murder of a young drugs dealer the previous December after a key witness refused to testify, was hit in the chest, arms and legs. One 27-year-old was hit in the mouth, while bullets grazed another man of the same age. Two of the victims were critically injured.

Seventy-year-old Ingeborg Tipping, who chaired the Whalley Range Association and had lived there for 44 years, was walking her young Alsatian, Santer, in the forecourt of her villa a few hundred yards from the pub, when the dog barked at a teenager on a mountain bike. The teenager turned and pulled a pistol from under his anorak.

'He pointed it at me and said "You're dead" – cheeky little git – and then made off,' she said. 'I do not mince my words ... if I could catch him I'd give him a hiding. But that's the way this area has gone – lawless. When we came here it was the place to live, but now....'

As far as anyone could see, the situation was only going to get worse. When the gangsters rounded up in Operation China were back out on the streets, open warfare was expected to break out – with the Goochies getting the worst of it. But that is not how things turned out. After an initial summit, representatives of the Crips and the Bloods flew in from Los Angeles to broker peace. The two famous rival gangs from South Central LA had a truce of their own at the time in the wake of the beating of black motorist Rodney King.

The ceasefire in Manchester lasted for two years. It was broken on 30 December 1995, when Raymond 'Pitbull' Pitt, the head of the Doddington Gang, was shot dead at point-blank range. His driver, 17-year-old Marios Baama, was wounded in the leg. Twenty-two-year-old Darrell Laycock was questioned about the killing, but released without charge. A week later Laycock and a woman friend were attacked in Moss Side by three men who fired 27 shots at them from handguns and a shotgun. Laycock was wearing a flak jacket but was wounded in the arm and head. Both survived and were kept under armed guard in hospital. During the investigation into the shooting, the police picked up a 13-year-old boy with £1,300 in his back pocket.

In 1996, the Young Gooch, an offshoot of the Gooch gang, gained a formidable reputation for gun violence. On 23 October, 17-year-old Orville Bell was sitting in his car in Longsight with a 15-year-old female friend when two gunmen approached. They were in their early teens and wearing bandanas. They fired two shots. One hit Bell in the throat. He died in hospital six days later after his family gave permission for his life-support machine to be turned off. It was no secret that the Young Gooch were responsible for the slaying. The murder also alerted the police to a new faction – the Longsight Crew. Civil war was about to break out.

The situation was all the more dangerous, as each generation of gang members was wilder than the one before. Raymond Pitt's younger brother Tommy, who had been in a young offenders' institution at the time of his brother's murder, was the baddest of them all. Gang life was all he knew.

When he was released in 1999, he found his faction of the Doddington Gang in disarray, reeling from attacks by other gangs. Through force of personality, his drive to avenge his brother and his utter ruthlessness, Tommy forged a new and incomparably more deadly gang. They were younger than south Manchester hoods, more naive and pliable, and Pitt could bend them to his will. He called his followers the Pitt Bull Crew – or the PBC – in memory of his dead brother. Tit-for-tat gang shootings increased dramatically. In 1999, there was a total of 81 shooting incidents across Greater Manchester, 68 per cent in south Manchester.

While Tommy Pitt blamed the older elements of the Doddington Gang for his brother's death, he initially turned his venom on the Longsight Crew, who seemed to be expanding their drug dealing into what he considered his turf. Pitt's team cruised in pairs on mountain bikes delivering heroin, cocaine and cannabis. One of them was an enforcer who carried a gun. They wore dark clothing. Their hoods were pulled over their heads to hinder identification. Under their jackets they wore bulletproof vests. On their gun hand, they wore a single golf glove so that police couldn't get fingerprints or traces of DNA from their weapons.

With the emergence of the PBC, south-central Manchester now had four main gangs. They were connected by an elaborate series of alliances and feuds. Simply put, Longsight and most of the Doddington gang were at war with the Gooch and the Pitt Bulls. Their killing grounds covered a semicircular patch around the city centre, from Openshaw in the east to Old Trafford in the west, and extending as far south as Levenshulme. Each gang had a core of main players, along with 'ordinary members' and the 'runners' who delivered drugs on behalf of members. Then there were a number of 'associates' who provided safe houses or kept guns. Some had connections with more than one gang. One gang survey estimated that they had around 200 members or associates, all under the age of 25. The Gooch numbered around 64, the Doddington 30, PBC 26 and the Longsight Crew 67. The PBC was the youngest gang, with one in five of its members aged 16 or under.

In March 2000, some Pitt Bulls were at a party with the Doddington when a gunfight broke out. One of the PBC was wounded. A few days later two of the Longsight Crew were shot in Gorton, probably by the Pitt Bulls. On 5 May, a car-load of PBC had a shoot-out with two members of the Longsight Crew in a vehicle in Prout Street, Longsight.

Things quickly escalated. Ten days later the bodies of Clifton Bryan and Denis Wilson were found in the boot of a car in the Harehills district of Leeds. Bryan was a Manchester gangster who had moved to Leeds. Wilson was a member of the Doddington Gang. They had been shot in the back of the head.

Meanwhile, the struggle between the PBC and the

Longsight Crew intensified. Many young men were too scared to attend the Moss Side carnival that summer. On 3 September, the Pitt Bulls shot Devon Bell in Langport Avenue, the Longsight Crew's base. Six days later, Pitt made another foray into Longsight territory. He shot and killed 21-year-old Marcus Greenidge and injured three others. The other two had a lucky escape when his Mac-10 machine gun jammed.

In mid-September a Longsight gunman saw Pitt in a car waiting at the traffic lights in the Victoria Park area. He cycled up and fired into the vehicle with a Mac-10. Pitt was hit in the leg and survived, but he was taken to Manchester Royal Infirmary where he was kept under armed guard in a secure unit. This gave the police a chance to observe him at close quarters.

'Pitt is a small lad but he has presence,' said one officer. 'Most [people you protect] you get a rapport with. They tend to be all right once they are with you; they might want a cigarette break or whatever and so they want to stay onside with you. Even though they are lying they will be all right. But Pitt, you just couldn't get into. If you were getting along with him, he would suddenly stop. It was amazing, this presence he had.'

Pitt was released, but he was not back on the streets for long. The police began arresting members of his gang. In raids on Pitt Bull strongholds, they recovered guns, ammunition, balaclavas, body armour, golf gloves and large quantities of heroin and crack. Pitt was arrested at a house in Hulme in November. The combat trousers he was wearing carried traces of shotgun residue. The police managed then to persuade 24-year-old Joshua 'Slips'

Mensah to testify against his own gang. This unprecedented breach in the code of silence was a crucial breakthrough. Pitt was convicted of murder and attempted murder, and sentenced to life.

The arrest of the Pitt Bull Crew was the first success of Operation Chrome, a £500,000 operation inspired by the success of an anti-gang initiative in Boston, Massachusetts. This had employed academic research to make a strategic study of the gangs involved, identifying their make-up and finding out what events triggered their feuds, before making a swoop.

But even with the Pitt Bulls off the street, the killing didn't stop. Between April 2001 and March 2002 there were eight fatal shootings, 84 serious woundings, 639 incidents of violence involving guns, 785 incidents of armed robbery, and 50 burglaries where guns were used. The war still centred on the Longsight Crew. In June 2001, 18-year-old Alan Byron was shot dead in Longsight. Two months later, 27-year-old Alphonso Madden was also gunned down. In October, Dean Eccleston was shot dead in Chorlton-on-Medlock. A few weeks later father-of-six George Lynch was shot dead after dropping off his son at a friend's house in Longsight. By the summer of 2002, Manchester had seen at least four more gang-related murders – two in a single weekend. That year, in confirmed gang-related incidents, there were five murders and 22 woundings using firearms. The youngest victim of gang-related gun violence was a 14-year-old boy; the eldest a 70-year-old woman caught in the crossfire of a gang shoot-out.

While making highly publicised 'crackdowns', the Operation Chrome team also brought in other agencies to tackle related problems from housing policy to street lighting and school exclusions. It was soon realised that gangs thrived in areas where the community was weak. A movement called Gangstop was launched by two friends, Michael McFarquhar and Gary Gordon. In the summer of 2002, they organised a march through Longsight, Rusholme, Moss Side, Hulme and Manchester's city centre. Some 400 marchers brought traffic to a standstill. They were joined by a group called Mothers Against Violence, who gave impassioned speeches about the loved ones they had lost.

That October Pitt went on trial at Preston Crown Court charged with the murders of Marcus Greenidge and Thomas Ramsey, and the attempted murder of three other men. Eleven others faced related conspiracy charges, along with two women who were accused of possessing guns.

Twenty-four-year-old Pitt was sentenced to life for the murder of Greenidge, with a further 20 for three attempted murders and 15 years for conspiracy.

'He is an infinitely cruel person in my view,' said the judge, Justice Michael Sachs. 'He is obsessed with his own importance and power.'

Warren Coudjoe, Gregory Day, Mark Simons, and Douglas and Sandra Thorne were convicted of conspiracy to possess firearms and plotting to deal drugs, while Moses Boakye, Stefan Proverbs, and a 16-year-old youth who could not be named for legal reasons admitted firearms and drugs offences. At a later trial, Paul 'Casper' Day, Abdul Butt and Mikey Gordon were jailed for life for the murder of a Longsight taxi driver. This marked the end of the Pitt Bull Crew.

It was not quite the end of Pitt's criminal career, though. The following year, 22-year-old legal secretary Lesley Darbyshire was sentenced to three-years' imprisonment for trying to smuggle fifty grams of heroin into his cell at Whitemoor high-security prison; it was concealed in her underwear.

In February 2003, the Attorney General, Lord Goldsmith, QC, appeared before the Court of Appeal and argued that the jail terms handed out to the Pitt Bull Crew were 'unduly lenient'. Lord Goldsmith had only once previously appeared in person to present a case. In four of the nine PBC cases, the appeal judges increased the jail terms. However, Pitt himself was already serving the maximum possible sentence.

Even without the Pitt Bulls, the war continued on the streets of south-central Manchester. After a drive-by shooting in April 2004, members of the rival Gooch and Longsight Crew gangs rampaged through the Manchester Royal Infirmary waving their guns in the air and causing panic and mayhem.

In 2006, 15-year-old Jessie James was shot dead as he cycled through Broadfield Park in Moss Side, a haunt of the Gooch Close Gang. He was returning from a party with his friends when he was cut down by a hail of bullets fired by a gunman hidden in the bushes. Hearing the gunshots, his friends fled. As Jessie lay dying on a grass verge, the killer approached and finished him off with more shots from a semi-automatic pistol.

Later, Jessie's friends returned to look for him. Unable to find Jessie, they rang his mobile phone and followed the sound of its ringing in the dark until they came across his dead body. Jessie's mother, Barbara Reid, believed that he had been killed because he refused to join a gang. Youngsters were expected to pledge allegiance to either the Gooch or Doddington gangs in their ongoing turf war. In Moss Side, the name of his alleged killer was widely known by most of the estate's largely Somali population, but despite the lure of a £20,000 reward and witness protection, no one is willing to speak to the police.

At the inquest, one witness has described how the teenager had become a marked man after he was fingered wrongly as a member of the rival Doddington Gang in front of the Gooch boys.

'They said to him "choose" but he didn't want to,' said Barbara Reid. 'He wanted to be everybody's friend. But they said that if he did not choose there is going to be enough blood around here. Three days later Jessie was dead.'

The gangs had made Jessie's life a living hell.

His mother said, 'Jessie was cornered, pointed out and intimidated at every opportunity. He was coerced and compelled to join the gang. Time and time again Jessie humiliated the gangsters to their faces by saying no to the gang. He said, "I don't want to join the gang. All I want to be is Jessie." This infuriated them and because they could not stand his rejection, they killed him. He was shot repeatedly and left to die alone like an animal ... I am told Jessie showed incredible strength when challenged by the gangsters who took his life because they could not stand a 15-year-old boy's rejection.'

Jessie's mother also said that his blood 'is on the hands of the murderer, his accomplices, their families and their friends ... who say nothing or do nothing.'

Jessie's killer has never been brought to trial. He was the twenty-fourth person to be shot dead in Moss Side since 1999.

By the mid-2000s, up to 30 competing gangs had sprung up in the area south of Manchester's city centre. Newcomers included the OT Cripz from Old Trafford, Rusholme Cripz and Fallowfield Mad Dogs, all of which claimed affiliation to the Gooch Gang. Members of these newer gangs already held grudges against the Young Longsight Soldiers, Young Doddington Crew and MSB – the Moss Side Bloodz. These in turn claimed ties to the original Doddington Crew. They inhabited what the press began calling the Triangle of Death: an area south-east of the city centre comprising Longsight, Hulme, Chorlton-on-Medlock and Moss Side. In some places, their territories were separated by the width of a single road.

At 1pm on 2 February 2007, a member of the Old Trafford Cripz was shot on Shrewsbury Street in Old Trafford. In retaliation, the Gooch Gang moved to Pepperhill Road, the centre of Doddington territory. At around 8pm, there was a shoot-out around the corner on Wilcock Street. When police arrived, they found nine bullet casings, one discharged bullet, one bullet fragment and three abandoned bicycles. The marks of bullet-strikes on Wilcock Street showed there had been a Wild West-style shoot-out with the two opposing groups at either end of the road.

The police also found a single trainer. Moments later, other officers saw youths running into Bold Street, on the Gooches' 'turf'. One was limping badly. They entered a house. Inside, police found Kayael Wint with gunshot wounds to his leg. He was wearing only one trainer. It matched the one that had already been recovered. He was also wearing body armour.

Later that evening, Narada Williams approached an ambulance that was parked at the junction of Alexandra Road South and Yarburgh Street, near Wilcock Street. He had a gunshot wound to his right foot. As he was being treated, a bullet fell out of his sock. Forensic analysis of the bullets showed that Wint and Williams had been hit by bullets from the same weapon. It was thought to have been a converted Russian Baikal self-loading pistol. A teenager named Tyler Mullings later admitted to owning one of the abandoned bicycles but denied any part in the shooting.

At the time, the Gooches were headed by 27-year-old Colin Joyce and 31-year-old Lee Amos. They had an efficient drug distribution operation. Drugs would be purchased in bulk from sources in Liverpool and Manchester, then repackaged into street-deal amounts and given to the gang's street dealers who had to pay protection money. Customers were given specific instructions where to meet, while suppliers would use taxis or hire cars to disguise their activities from the police. Gang member made considerable profits, which they used to fund their champagne lifestyles. Violence was used to maintain discipline. Low-level members of the gang were threatened or savagely beaten if they disobeyed orders.

At 6.45pm on 15 June 2007, 24-year-old Ucal Chin, a member of the Longsight Crew, was driving his red Renault Megane along Anson Road with two friends. A silver Audi pulled up alongside; a passenger in the rear seat wound down the window. He fired seven shots into the Megane. Three bullets hit Ucal in the chest, back and right arm. They ripped through his liver, heart and lungs, causing massive internal bleeding.

Ucal was no longer able to control the car. It swerved and crashed into an electrical box. Paramedics from the nearby Manchester Royal Infirmary rushed to the scene, but there was little they could do. Ucal died in hospital soon after.

His funeral took place on 27 July. At about 10pm, a number of mourners went to Chin's family home in Frobisher Close, Chortlon-on-Medlock for a wake. Among them were a number of members of the Longsight Crew and the Doddington Gang. For the Gooch Gang, it was too good an opportunity to miss.

Shortly before midnight, a number of people from the wake were standing outside the house when a Honda Legend, a blue Audi and another silver car drove down Frobisher Close. The windows of the Honda were wound down. Gunmen sprayed bullets indiscriminately into the crowd. Terrified children screamed as bullets ricocheted off the walls. Twenty-three-year-old Tyrone Gilbert, a close friend of Chin's, was hit in the chest by a single bullet. It penetrated his heart, liver and right lung. Gilbert died in hospital later. Another friend was hit twice in the left leg and the cars outside were peppered with bullet holes. Police forensic experts later determined that the gunmen had used two revolvers and a 9mm semi-automatic pistol.

As the three cars sped away, they kept their lights off. A police car spotted them and gave chase but – at the high speeds they reached – could not keep up. At Firethorn

Avenue the Honda was abandoned. Some of the occupants fled to the Audi. Two other men were seen running behind the third car. One of them jumped over a fence, apparently looking for somewhere to hide. As he jumped back his balaclava snagged on barbed wire. Leaving it behind, he and his accomplice ran from Firethorn Avenue across Avon Road and into the driveway of the flats opposite. A police officer saw one of the men running across the road and went to investigate, but the men climbed over another fence out of sight. However, in Firethorn Avenue the policeman found the abandoned Honda and the balaclava.

Saliva around the mouth-hole of the balaclava yielded enough DNA to link it to 25-year-old Aeeron Campbell, a known gang member. Distinctive blue fibres found on the balaclava and the car seats provided a strong scientific link between the headgear and the Honda. Further tests on the Honda found high levels of gun discharge residue of different types, indicating that at least one gun had been fired from the car.

Mobile phone data showed Joyce and Amos had been talking to each other immediately before Ucal's murder, and the location of Joyce's phone was consistent with the route taken by the Audi. The two men had been released on licence only three months before, after being jailed for nine years for firearm offences. Further analysis of mobile phone data suggested that Joyce, Amos and Ricardo Williams were in one of the cars used in the shooting of Tyrone Gilbert and that Narada Williams was co-ordinating the operation from a safe location. Once the Honda had been abandoned on Firethorn Avenue, phone records showed that Joyce and Amos were in a vehicle heading for Stockport. Ricardo Williams was also in a car that went to Ashton-under-Lyne. Narada Williams continued to liaise with the other members of the team and remained a central point of contact.

It was plain that the murders were linked and pre-planned. In the days after Ucal died, Narada Williams was known to have sent someone to buy dark clothing to use in a 'drive-by'. And the cars involved had been bought for the purpose; they had tinted windows.

A few days after the shooting at the wake, one of the gang's associates read about the drive-by in the newspaper and recognised the description of the Honda. It was bought on 17 July and he had been asked to look after it. He called Narada Williams who told him to burn the logbook.

Between August 2007 and May 2008, the suspects were arrested one by one. Having determined the gang's command structure, it became clear to the investigators that the gang had overstretched themselves in extending their drug dealing operations to Moston, Stalybridge and Ashton-under-Lyne, where they could not expect the loyalty they could command on their inner-city turf. This allowed the police to persuade low-level street dealers to give evidence in exchange for protection. Six witnesses, all former associates of the gang, were given immunity from prosecution and, on 5 November, the police recovered the charred remains of the logbook, along with a spare key.

During the investigation, a number of uniformed police officers were giving a talk on the dangers of gun crimes in the Moss Side Leisure Centre when three Gooch boys barged into the gym next door. In the weights room, 21-year-old Antonio Wint, 22-year-old Andre Marshall and an unidentified teenager singled out 23-year-old Soloman Sullivan who was involved in a feud with Kayael Wint. They hit him several times before Wint cocked a 9mm sub-machine gun, pointed it at Sullivan and threatened to shoot him. Instead, he pistol-whipped him with the weapon.

Alerted by other gym users, the police called in an armed response unit. The gunmen escaped in a green Subaru, but were spotted leaving an address in Whalley Range some 20 minutes later. As police gave chase, Wint was seen throwing a plastic bag over a nearby wall. It was later discovered to contain a gun. After a brief chase through the alleyways of Whalley Range they were arrested.

At Manchester Crown Court in May 2008, Antonio Wint was jailed for an indeterminate period after pleading guilty to possessing a firearm – the Czech-made Scorpion machine gun – with intent to endanger life. Marshall was imprisoned for seven years after pleading guilty to assault and possessing a prohibited firearm. The 17-year-old, who accompanied them and could not be identified, pleaded guilty to violent disorder and was ordered to complete a community punishment sentence.

Detective Sergeant Rick Collins said: 'These three offenders armed themselves and walked calmly into a busy gym in the middle of the day with no regard for people's safety. Their arrogance is astonishing, but we have proved they are not above the law, and our streets are safer now they are in jail.'

In December 2008, Joyce, Amos and nine other members of the Gooch Gang began a five-month trial before Liverpool Crown Court. The court was told that, together, they had embarked on a plan to expand heroin and cocaine dealing across the city's suburbs, using torture to control street dealers while 'rubbing out' potential rivals. Their arsenal of weapons included machine guns and magnum-style handguns, which they used 'at the drop of a hat' to exact revenge and enforce drug debts. They would shoot at people over minor disagreements while drunk in nightclubs, and torture street dealers who crossed them, the court heard. The evidence came from former gang members who were, by then, on the Witness Protection Programme.

The 11 were convicted of 27 of the 28 charges against them, including the drive-by killing of Tyrone Gilbert at the wake for Ucal Chin, who Joyce had murdered a few weeks earlier.

'You were all involved in gang-related activity which is all too reminiscent of Al Capone and Chicago in the era of prohibition,' said Judge Brian Langstaff. 'Manchester is not the Wild West, but many of you treated its streets as if it were.'

In a show of bravado, Joyce smirked throughout the judge's remarks and was applauded by other gang members in the dock as he told the court that the trial had been a circus, and that no sentence could take away the 'freedom and innocence from inside me'.

Joyce was found guilty of murdering both Chin and Gilbert. Judge Langstaff admitted that Joyce possessed 'considerable personal charm', organisational ability and business skills – the court had heard that he made up to £700,000 a year from drug dealing and lived in a luxury flat in Worsley. However, he also had 'murderous intent' and was a 'deeply controlling man'.

'I accept undoubtedly you are a leader of men,' the judge said.

Joyce was given two life sentences and told he must serve a minimum of 39 years. He was told that he would be an old-age pensioner before he would be considered for release. His second-in-command, Lee Amos, was also convicted of killing Tyrone Gilbert. He was sentenced to life imprisonment and ordered to serve a minimum of 35 years.

Twenty-five-year-old Aeeron Campbell, a thug with an intelligence that put him in the bottom one per cent of the population, was given life with a minimum of 32 years before parole. Known as 'Yardie', 27-year-old Narada Williams, a gang 'enforcer' in charge of their drugs operation, was given life with a minimum of 35 years. Twenty-six-year-old Ricardo Williams, also convicted of murder, was jailed for life with a minimum of 34 years. Hassan Shah, 25, who went down for firearms and drugs offences, was given an indefinite sentence, but must serve at least nine years.

Judge Langstaff told the defendants: 'Your reactions to the verdicts suggest to me you could not care less. It as almost as if you regarded the badge of a guilty verdict as being a mark of honour in the cause for which you had shot.'

Six other members of the gang were locked up for offences including gun possession and drug dealing. Twenty-two-year-old Aaron Alexander got 13 years; 21-year-old Ricci Moss received six. Twenty-year-old Kayael Wint must serve at least five-and-a-half years. Eighteen-year-old Tyler Mullings was given six years in a young offenders' institution. Twenty-five-year-old Gonoo Hussain pleaded guilty to his part in the conspiracy. He admitted he was a driver for the gang when members supplied their drugs and was present when guns were picked up from various hideouts. He got five-and-a-half years.

Since their arrest, Greater Manchester Police have recorded a 92 per cent reduction in gun-related crime. With both the Gooches and Doddingtons behind bars after a 20-year reign of terror, the police began Operation Cougar to take guns off the streets. Officers from the Greater Manchester Xcalibre Organised Crime Unit descended in overwhelming numbers without warning to arrest youths targeted by plain-clothed police patrolling in unmarked cars.

Peter Fahy, the Chief Constable of Greater Manchester Police, said: 'Our next step is to identify the next generation of gang members and stop them from falling into this sort of lifestyle. What we have to understand is what drives these young people to embark on this lifestyle in the first place. The communities have the best understanding of how to tackle this issue and, by continuing to work and build relationships with them, we want to educate young people about the consequences of getting involved in the first place. The police cannot do this alone. Now is the time to step up and take responsibility, and stop the sort of tragedies that resulted in the deaths of young men like Ucal Chin and Tyrone Gilbert from happening.'

For over a year, there were no fatal shootings. The police even talked optimistically about the 'end of gang culture'. Then shortly before midnight on Sunday, 12 May 2009, 16-year-old Giuseppe Gregory was killed by a gunman who sprayed bullets at a green VW Golf as it left the car park of the Robin Hood pub in Stretford. It had all the hallmarks of a gangland slaying.

CHAPTER 4

THE ESSEX BOYS

The Essex Boys were one of the most feared gangs of the 1990s. Their reputation for violence meant that few people were likely to report them to the police. They first came to public attention in 1995, following the death of Essex schoolgirl Leah Betts. She took a tablet of ecstasy on her eighteenth birthday and fell into a coma. Four days later she was pronounced dead and her life-support system was turned off. The ecstasy had been supplied by the Essex Boys. Three weeks later, a trio of leading members of the gang were found dead in a Range Rover parked in a dirty track near Rettendon in Essex. Each had been killed by a shotgun blast to the head. Surviving gang member Bernard O'Mahoney told the story of the gang's rise and fall in the book *Essex Boys*. The book was made into a film of the same name, starring Sean Bean, and O'Mahoney has gone on to establish himself as a writer.

Bernard O'Mahoney moved to Essex in 1986, after

serving a short sentence in prison for wounding. He had cut a man with a bottle during an argument in a pub in his hometown of Wolverhampton. He fled to South Africa but was arrested and jailed on his return. On his release he decided to make a fresh start and moved in with his girlfriend Debra, a hairdresser from Basildon. O'Mahoney got a job driving for a haulage firm in East London. Within three years, they had two children and were having a hard time making ends meet, so O'Mahoney began working as a doorman at nightclubs during evenings and weekends. On the recommendation of Reggie Kray, he got a job at Raquel's nightclub in Basildon and rose to become head of security there. In that role, he controlled who could sell drugs in the club. Approved dealers had to pay upfront; those who did not were 'discouraged'.

Through Raquel's, O'Mahoney got to know local hard man Tony Tucker who provided security for a number of clubs in Essex and London. A friend of former middleweight boxing champion Nigel Benn, Tucker supplied bouncers and backup if it was required. Otherwise O'Mahoney was left to his own devices. In return, Tucker made money from the club, supplying drugs, protection and dodgy invoices.

The 'firm' quickly established a reputation and their services were much in demand. They provided protection, collected debts and delivered punishment beatings. Some of their work was actually legal. They protected a local Asian lad from his in-laws when he tried to break off an arranged marriage. In another case, O'Mahoney went to collect a debt from a cab driver who then died in a mysterious hit-and-run accident outside his own home; the car was found burnt out soon after. O'Mahoney denied having anything to do with the cabbie's death. The man only owed £800, too small an amount for their firm to murder someone for. They were accused, however, and then in turn fined the man who had commissioned them £3,000 for giving their names to the police.

For £500 they torched another man's car. The driver had driven up and down outside a neighbour's house, revving his engine and playing loud music. The screech of tyres got on the neighbour's nerves – so much so that he paid the firm to put a stop to it.

The firm also provided protection at drug deals. They acted as minders, saying and doing nothing unless the deal went sour. Then extreme violence would be employed.

O'Mahoney and his men quickly learnt that there was as much money to be made from failing to collect a debt as from collecting it. They would ask a client for expenses to be paid upfront. Then they would keep going back for more, while making no effort to contact the debtor. When clients got wise to that, they stopped taking money upfront but said simply that they would keep a third of anything they collected. However, if the client cancelled the contract, he would still owe the firm a third of the money outstanding. They would then intimidate the person who owed the money. The debtor would phone the police who, in turn, would call the person the money was owed to and threaten to prosecute them unless they called off their debt collectors. With the contract thus terminated, the firm then asked the customer for their money.

At Raquel's, O'Mahoney and Tucker made an effort to move the club up-market. They cleared out the drunks and peroxide blondes and turned it into a venue for house and garage music. This attracted young, middle-class ravers, whose drug of choice was ecstasy. The firm made sure 'E' was freely available.

With this success under his belt, O'Mahoney expanded his circle of criminal acquaintances. He was at Tucker's birthday party at the Prince of Wales pub in South Ockenden where he was hit in the back by the door as someone barged in. When the intruder failed to apologise, O'Mahoney said, 'You've just knocked the fucking door into me.'

'Well, you're a doorman, aren't you,' came the reply.

Sensing a fight was about to break out, Tucker stepped in and introduced the newcomer as his close friend Craig Rolfe.

Six months later another of Tucker's close associates, body-builder Pat Tate, returned to Basildon after serving four years of a six-year sentence. After a row about the bill in a nearby Happy Eater, Tate had helped himself to the contents of the till. When he was arrested, he was found to be in possession of cocaine. In court, fearing that he was going to prison, he leapt from the dock and ran for the door, injuring a policeman and a WPC on the way. Once outside he made off on a motorbike, and surfaced some time later in Spain. But, foolishly, after a year, he decided to visit Gibraltar, where he was promptly arrested and shipped back to England. Now that he was out he was recruited by the firm, along with Steve 'Nipper' Ellis from Southend.

Tucker and Tate passed the time coming up with increasingly ambitious ways to smuggle drugs into the country. Simultaneously, their own consumption soared, making them unpredictable and dangerous. One day they were in a 7-Eleven in Southend with Ellis when they started throwing food at one another. Tucker and Tate walked out but Ellis was arrested. The incident in itself was trivial, but in Tucker's drug-addled mind it became all-too-serious.

The following day, Tucker turned up at Ellis's house with Rolfe, put a gun to his head and threatened to kill him for grassing him up over the food fight. They then discussed hacking off Ellis's feet and hands with a machete. In the end, they simply trashed Nipper's house, smearing shit on everything they didn't steal.

The next day a brick was thrown through Tate's window. When he came out to find out what was going to, Ellis shot him, smashing the bones of his elbow. Ellis was convicted of possessing a firearm and sentenced to seven-and-a-half months in jail, where he received constant death threats.

Tate, meanwhile, was in hospital. Members of the firm gathered around his bed, taking drugs and listening to loud house music. It was a non-stop party. No one dared object. Then a nurse found a gun under Tate's pillow when she was making the bed and called the police. Tate was sent back to prison for breaking the conditions of his parole. Paranoia began to spread through the firm. Tucker would drive around in his Porsche with a handgun on the seat between his legs. O'Mahoney kept one gun under the dashboard of his car, another in the boot. He had more scattered around his home so that he would never be out of reach of one if he needed it.

Rolfe introduced Tucker to another Basildon boy, Kevin Whittaker. Whittaker was used in a £60,000 drug deal with an outfit in Romford. It went wrong and Whittaker lost Tucker's £60,000. Tucker and Rolfe force-fed Whittaker cocaine and ketamine – 'Special K' – until he was unconscious then left him in the middle of the road. After they drove off, Rolfe thought better off it and persuaded Tucker to stop the car. He got out, ran back and tried to rouse his old mate. When that did not work, they slung him in the back of the car, drove down a side road and dumped his corpse in a ditch. When he was found, the police assumed that he was a junkie who had died of an overdose.

Soon after Tate got out of jail, a story appeared in the local press concerning £500,000-worth of cannabis found in a farmer's pond in Rettendon, Essex, just seven miles from Basildon. It appeared that it had been dropped from a small plane but had missed the drop zone in a nearby field and ended up in the duck pond.

Tucker was not happy that other people were doing drugs deals in what he considered his territory. He heard that the lost cannabis had been on its way to a mob in Canning Town. He put out the word that he wanted to be informed when a new shipment was coming in so that he could buy into the deal. In fact, he intended to steal it.

Meanwhile, he was funding an operation bringing in drugs from Amsterdam, packed in cars where the only people substantially at risk were the drivers, who were paid around £7,000 a trip. The operation was run by Darren Nicholls, someone Tate had met in prison. However, half the cannabis turned out to be duff. Tucker was out of £120,000 and Nicholls was in hot water.

Things were about to get a great deal worse. On 11

November 1995, Leah Betts was celebrating her eighteenth birthday in Raquel's when she took an 'E' and collapsed. The following day, the Essex Boys were suffering a lot of unwelcome attention from the police and the press. O'Mahoney complained that people he had known for years had stopped speaking to him, while others tried to trick him into supplying them with drugs in the hope of making him the fall guy.

Tucker and Tate went to Amsterdam to get the £120,000. The money, in fact, belonged to the local drugs syndicate, but Tucker and Tate kept it and blamed Nicholls for blowing the drug deal and pocketing the money. Nicholls, they assumed, would soon be dead. But he was not the only one in trouble. O'Mahoney knew that the Canning Town mob were not an outfit to be trifled with and tried to distance himself from Tucker's plan to rip them off. He quit his job at Raquel's. As a result, he received a threatening phone call from Tucker who accused him of disloyalty. Then the police called O'Mahoney, telling him he was in danger. Tucker was out to get him.

Everything was now prepared for the drug heist. Tucker and Tate had bought a machine gun and silencer. They had also recruited a small player in the Canning Town mob who called on 6 December, informing them that the next shipment would be dropped near Rettendon the following evening. He arranged to meet them so he could show them where the drop was going to be. Tucker, Tate and Rolfe drove out to meet him that night.

At 8am the following morning, two local men were going out to feed the pheasants in nearby fields when they saw a metallic blue Range Rover parked in Workhouse

Lane, near Rettendon. They stopped their Land Rover and got out. As they walked past the Range Rover, one of the men glanced inside. He saw three men and, not realising they were dead, he tapped on the window.

'For all the world they looked as though they had fallen asleep in the car,' he said. 'It wasn't until I looked again that I realised they had been shot. I was shocked; it was not something I expected to find. The driver was lying with his head on one side and blood coming out of his nose.'

They had been taken completely by surprise in a classic gangland killing. The driver, Rolfe, was still holding the steering wheel. Only a broken rear nearside window, apparently smashed by a shot, gave any external indication that anything untoward had taken place. However, the lane was well known to the local criminal fraternity. A hijacked cigarette lorry was taken there six years before. And a safe, the proceeds of another crime, had been found dumped there more recently.

Initially both O'Mahoney and Nipper Ellis were suspects. Ellis told the *Sun*: 'It wasn't me who did it, but I'd love to shake the hand of the man who did. He's my hero.'

However, 53-year-old engineer Michael Steele and 33-year-old mechanic Jack Whomes were arrested for the murders. They were associates of Darren Nicholls, who claimed to have been the unwitting getaway driver that night. Nicholls had turned Queen's evidence after being charged with conspiracy to import cannabis.

The trial at the Old Bailey in 1999 lasted almost five months and cost an estimated £1.5 million. Protection for supergrass Darren Nicholls and his family alone was thought to have cost more than £300,000. Even the judge,

Mr Justice Hidden, noted that the prosecution case rested entirely on Nicholls's evidence.

On the day of the murders, Nicholls said he had met Steele and Whomes, who he had known for a couple of years, at around 5pm. He said he was told they were going to meet Tate and the others regarding a drug deal. The rendezvous was the Halfway House pub near Rettendon. They would drive there in convoy. Whomes and Nicholls went in Nicholls's VW Passat, while Steele drove his Toyota Hilux.

At the Halfway House, the Passat was parked out of sight when the Range Rover carrying Tucker, Tate and Rolfe swept into the car park. Steele got out of the Hilux and got into the back of the Range Rover with Tate. They drove away.

Whomes changed into a boiler suit and Wellington boots then directed Nicholls who drove him to the end of Workhouse Lane. There, Whomes got out of the car and said he would phone when he needed to be picked up. The call came at 7pm. Nicholls said he was told to 'come and get us'. It was only when he saw the two men's blood-spattered surgical gloves after they got into the car that he realised what had happened, Nicholls claimed.

He said that the killers had laughed over how one of the victims had 'squealed like a baby' as he tried to escape death. Nicholls said Steele had boasted, 'I have done everyone a favour. I am the Angel of Death. I have got rid of people who were not the kind you would want to have around.'

Based on Nicholls's testimony, the prosecution came up with a theory. After being dropped off by Nicholls, the prosecution maintained that Whomes had hidden in the bushes and waited for the Range Rover to arrive. Tate, Tucker and Rolfe, guided by Steele, drove unsuspectingly down Workhouse Lane, thinking they were on a reconnaissance trip. At the end of the lane, there was a locked gate. The prosecution contended that Steele had told the others he had a key and got out of the Range Rover, ostensibly to open the gate. As prearranged, Whomes came out of hiding, handed a gun to Steele and the slaughter commenced.

Later O'Mahoney saw the photographs of the crime scene and summarised what had happened.

'Craig Rolfe, the driver, was the first to die,' O'Mahoney said. 'He looked as if he had pulled up at traffic lights. He was slumped to one side, with blood running from his nose and mouth. His eyes were closed. His hands were still on the steering wheel. Tony Tucker was in the passenger seat. He had been the second to die. He was sitting bolt upright, his head bowed. He had blood all over his face and chest. Pat Tate was slumped across the back seat, his head lying in the broken window. Blood spilled from his chin onto his chest.'

Each victim had been shot twice in the chest. Tate had also been shot in the stomach and head. Curiously, given the circumstances, they were not armed.

'None was wearing seat belts and none had weapons,' said O'Mahoney, 'which I thought was unbelievable for those three.'

It appeared that Tucker and Rolfe knew nothing about their imminent demise. Tate had tried to react, but a shot to the abdomen immobilised him. He had been finished off with another shot to the head. O'Mahoney maintained that he only heard of the murders when he got a message on his answerphone from a detective asking him to contact the police.

'We've found a Range Rover with three bodies inside,' said the detective. 'We think it's your mates.'

'Are they dead?' asked O'Mahoney.

'They're very dead,' came the reply.

According to Nicholls, the killers chuckled as they told him how Steele's gun had fallen apart as they opened fire.

'Mick told me Jack was a cold-hearted bastard because once Mick got out of the Range Rover, Jack shot them all immediately,' said Nicholls. 'Then he reloaded and without any emotion shot them all again in the back of the head.'

After being handed the pump-action shotgun, Steele shot all three men once again. In total eight shots were fired.

'They said they had done the world a favour by killing those men,' said Nicholls. 'Steele said, "Nobody will miss them. They deserved to die".'

However, both Steele and Whomes had alibis. Steele produced petrol and supermarket Visa receipts from 5pm on 6 December that showed he had been in Colchester at the time. What's more, he could not have been driving the Hilux that day as it took diesel.

His former sister-in-law, postmistress Phyllis Stambrook, testified that she had met Steele at his home at 7.30 that evening. But under cross-examination she said she could not be sure of the date.

Steele appeared in the witness box. Against legal advice, he told the jury of his long criminal record, largely involved with drug smuggling. He maintained that he was innocent and wanted to tell the jury of his previous convictions in an effort to be straight with them. This was not thought to have helped his case.

Whomes admitted he had been in the car park of the Halfway House that evening. He was a mechanic and he was collecting Nicholls's VW Passat, which had broken down. After loading it on his trailer, he phoned Nicholls to tell him he was on his way back to the yard.

The defence pointed out that the Passat had no heater, a noisy exhaust and a clutch that practically was unusable. This was hardly the car you would choose to make a getaway in on a cold winter night after a triple murder. What's more, this battered old Passat somehow went up and down Workhouse Lane without leaving any tyre tracks or oil leaks. Forensic tests on the car found no gun residues, or traces of blood and glass – or anything linking it to the murder scene.

Forensic engineer Ian Bristowe told the court that Whomes could not have made the call asking to be collected from Workhouse Lane, because his mobile phone would not work with either of the two aerials covering the crime scene.

Whomes was a big man – six-foot two-inches tall and weighing almost 19 stone. According to the prosecution he had secreted himself in the bushes by the gate at the end of the lane. Again, he had done this without leaving a trace. At the scene of the crime a single footprint was found by the offside rear door where the killer would have stood. It came from a 'hi-tech' trainer, size eight or nine. Whomes's feet were size eleven. Besides, according to Nicholls, he was wearing Wellington boots.

Nicholls also provided a motive. It was Steele, not him,

he said, that had made the deal for the duff cannabis in Amsterdam. So it was Steele who was in danger of being rubbed out by the syndicate after Tucker and Tate had pocketed the refund. Nicholls also said that Tate suspected that his girlfriend, Sarah Saunders, was having an affair with Steele. Nicholls said that Saunders told Steele that Tate knew of their entanglement and aimed to murder him. Saunders vehemently denied this.

Under cross-examination, Nicholls admitted that he had been an informer for a police officer, who was himself facing criminal charges. Asked if he was a 'truthful man by nature?' he replied, 'I don't think you could say I am.' Then he quickly insisted, 'I'm telling the truth now.'

Had he 'ever thought about what was honest and dishonest?' he was asked.

'Not particularly,' was his blithe reply.

He admitted that he knew Steele 'very well, and had the means to make up a plausible story about him and his colleagues,' explaining that he 'would have done anything to get Whomes and Steele arrested.' However, neither of them knew that Nicholls harboured ill feeling towards them.

Nicholls explained that, because of the murders, he was now terrified of them and hoped never to see either of the pair again.

'So, Mr Steele would hardly be on your Christmas card list?' asked Graham Parkins, QC.

'No,' said Nicholls.

'Can you explain, then,' asked Mr Parkins, 'why you sent his family a card for Christmas 1995?' This was just over a fortnight after the murders.

Indeed, two days after Christmas, Nicholls had taken his little daughters to Steele's house to watch the rabbits playing in the garden and had continued doing odd jobs and electrical work for Steele for the next few months. Nicholls only changed his tune when he was arrested in May 1996 while in possession of ten kilos of cannabis resin with a street value of £25,000. While on remand, he was given the VIP treatment. In his cell, he had a table and chairs, a wardrobe, colour TV and a multi-gym. Instead of subsisting on prison food, he was provided a takeaway service. One day he would have tacos, the next Kentucky Fried Chicken. He was even given hot chocolate at bedtime.

Police transcripts of his statements showed numerous instances where Nicholls appears to have been prompted or led. On some tapes he even appeared to be reading. It came out in court that the officers who interviewed Nicholls spent more than 30 hours in his cell with no tape recorder running. One of these un-taped interviews lasted nearly eight hours. Even Nicholls's solicitor thought this was unusual – even undesirable – while the police maintained they were merely making 'comfort visits'.

In his summing up, the judge counselled caution.

'Nicholls is a convicted criminal who was engaged in drug abuse and the importation of drugs into this country,' he told the jury. 'You must bear in mind it was in his own interest to become a prosecution witness ... he hopes to get less time to serve.'

Indeed, he was sentenced to just 15 months on the conspiracy charge and walked free as he had already served that time on remand.

Still, Nicholls's evidence secured Steele's and Whomes's

convictions. The jury were out for four-and-a-half days, but in the end returned a unanimous 'guilty' verdict. As a foreman delivered the verdict, three women jurors broke down and wept.

The judge had no option. On 20 January 1998, Justice Hidden sentenced Steele and Whomes to life, with a recommendation they serve a minimum of 15 years.

Under the Protected Witness Programme, Nicholls and his family were whisked away to start a new life with a new identity.

'Of all the supergrasses in the system, I am the tops,' he crowed.

Four months before Nicholls was arrested, the police had picked up Billy Jasper for armed robbery. He was an East End villain with fondness for crack cocaine and heroin. Well used to police interviews, he did not want to talk about the offence he had been arrested for. However, he was willing to talk about the Rettendon murders and confessed to being the getaway driver – though he, like Nicholls, said he did not know what was being planned.

In the autumn of 1995, Jasper said he had met a well-known villain called Jesse Gale at Moreton's Bar in Canning Town. They were joined by a third man, who has not been named for legal reasons. They moved on to a Mexican restaurant, where the conversation turned to Tucker, Tate and Rolfe. Tucker and Tate had a reputation for double-crossing people on drugs deals and it was clear that they intended to roll the Canning Town mob, who were determined not to let this happen. Gale and the unnamed suspect also had a personal score to settle with Tucker and Tate, who had ripped them off for

£20,000 in an earlier drug deal. While Gale simply wanted to rob Tucker and Tate, the unidentified man was to 'take them out of the game'. He offered Jasper £5,000 to drive for him.

On the night of 6 December, Jasper said he picked up a grey Fiat Uno Turbo from outside Peacock Gym in East London and drove to a bar near Hornchurch to pick up the unidentified man. He was carrying a heavy sports bag. They drove to Upminster Bridge where Jesse Gale was waiting outside the office of Windmill Cabs. Gale and the unidentified man disappeared down the side of the building. Soon after the latter reappeared alone, still carrying the sports bag.

Then they droved to Rettendon, where Jasper was directed to a drop-off point beside a lane. The unnamed man said he was going to pick up four kilos of cocaine. He returned about 40 minutes later, carrying a rucksack along with the sports bag. He was wearing surgical gloves, a blue tracksuit and Reebok trainers, around size eight or nine – like the print left outside the offside rear door. Then he phoned Gale and said that everything had been sorted. It was only then that Jasper glimpsed the 9mm Browning pistol and the sawn-off shotgun he was carrying. It was just past midnight.

Jasper said that he heard about the murders the next day and put two-and-two together. When Jasper went to meet the unnamed assassin at Moreton's Bar to collect his money, he said, 'You ****, you took them out of the game.' They were alone in the toilets doing a line of cocaine at the time. The suspect merely grinned and told Jasper not to ask questions.

The police did not follow up on Jasper's story. At the trial he was called by the defence, but the judge ruled that much of his evidence was inadmissible. After the trial, Jasper continued to stand by his story, but it could not be corroborated by Jesse Gale as he had died in a car crash in May 1998. Former associates said he was murdered.

Jasper's account fits much of the available evidence. However, the police put the time of death at around 7pm. That was the time the three victims stopped using their mobile phones – and the time fixed by Nicholls. Curiously, the police pathologist did not try and ascertain time of death by any of the normal methods.

'It didn't seem important,' she told the court.

Three local witnesses gave statements to the police saying they heard shots between 10pm and midnight that night. Another witness said he was taking his dog for a walk along Workhouse Lane at 7pm and he was positive that the blue Range Rover was not there then.

On the night of the murder it was cold. During the day it had snowed in Essex, but the Range Rover showed little sign of being left out all night when it was discovered early the next morning. That, again, would indicate that the murders took place later than Nicholls said.

Five months later, Tate's close friend John Marshall, who had been entrusted with £120,000 of drug money, was found dead under bales of straw in the boot of his car. The police have always insisted there is no link between the two crimes. But the case remains open and no one has ever been charged over Marshall's death. However, his name was linked to Brink's Mat bullion robber Kenneth Noye. Marshall, a car dealer, is thought to have supplied Noye with stolen licence plates. He went missing just days before Noye knifed 21-year-old Stephen Cameron to death on the M25 in a road-rage killing, for which he is now serving life. While doing time for the Brink's Mat heist, Noye palled up with Pat Tate, but Noye disliked Tate's drug-induced mood swings and fell out with him.

Despite their convictions, Steele and Whomes insisted they were innocent. During a five-day appeal in 2006, their lawyers argued that Nicholls had fabricated his entire story – with the help of police. Nicholls had signed a lucrative book deal based on the case before it even went to trial, a fact not known by the jury. The three appeal judges found that Nicholls's media contacts did not undermine the safety of the convictions. Lord Justice Maurice Kay said the allegations of police collusion were 'at best speculation'. The appeal was denied.

Steele's barrister, Baroness Helena Kennedy vowed to take the case to the House of Lords. She told the court: 'The judgment may be seen as licensing police misconduct.'

Before Steele was led back to the cells, he waved his fist at police from the dock and cried: 'You are a corrupt lot and you will not always have the bench to protect you.'

Steele and Whomes have no hope of any future parole because both men continue to maintain their innocence. Whomes has been described as a model prisoner. Illiterate when arrested, he taught himself to read and write by following the tapes and transcripts of Nicholls's evidence against him, and he continued to further his education.

He made a further attempt to establish his innocence by contacting journalist Jo-Ann Goodwin. Apologising for his misspellings, he wanted her to look into every detail of his past life so he could understand 'what they have done to me'.

Her investigation among the criminals of Canning Town confirmed much of what he had said.

Before his arrest, Whomes said he loved both his family and his work.

'I have a lovely wife, and two lovely kids,' he said. 'My wife is Gail, and we met at school. I have had a lot of wet pillows on my bed thinking about them.'

This is the man who was supposed to be a cold-blooded killer who calmly carried on blasting his victims as Steele's gun fell apart.

After the court case, the Range Rover in which the killings took place was released to the finance company by the police. In July 2000, it was for sale on eBay. The vendor said: 'It is a part of criminal history, like Bonnie and Clyde's car.'

CHAPTER 5

THE YARDIES

Originally Jamaican, the Yardies have strongholds in both north and south London, as well as Bristol, Birmingham and Nottingham. Importing drugs, they have contacts in the Caribbean, New York and Canada. With no centralised structure, they are often riven with internecine rivalries. Between 1986 and 1995, they were thought to have been responsible for 57 murders, including the cold-blooded murder of a policeman, though there were only considered to have between 80 and 200 Yardies in the country at the time. When Operation Trident, Scotland Yard's attempt to crush the Yardies, started in 2002, there had been 11 murders between January and June and five more in July.

Jamaican Yardies first established themselves in the UK in the 1980s. They quickly took control of the trade in illegal drugs, particularly marijuana and crack cocaine. There was little opposition as the Yardies soon gained a reputation for their use of guns. The term 'Yardie' comes from the slang for the inhabitants of the Trenchtown neighbourhood of Kingston Jamaica, where the government housing for returning servicemen was built around a central courtyard, or yard. In Jamaica the word is not applied to members of local gangs but to Jamaicans who have been gang members abroad and have returned home.

By 1987, blood-chilling reports reached the UK from the US, where agencies logged more than 600 Yardie murders in the previous three years and estimated they were earning up to $9 million per month per city from the sale of crack cocaine. In one chilling incident, a New York drug dealer tried to steal three ounces of cocaine from some Yardies. He was swiftly killed and his decapitated head was wrapped in masking tape and used in a celebratory game of football. That same year, they began making their presence felt in London, pumping crack cocaine into black housing estates and using guns and knives on the slightest pretext.

In 1981, Robert Blackwood had had a top ten hit in the UK with 'Fatty Boom Boom' under the name Rankin' Dread. Blackwood had been brought up in the districts of Rema and Tivoli in Kingston. In the 1970s, he became famous as a DJ on the Ray Symbolic sound system in Jamaica. He became involved with Jamaican gang leader Claude Massop and was wanted in connection with 30 murders before moving to London where he became 'number one Yardie godfather'. Living under several aliases, including Errol Codling, he became the head of a gang of drug dealers and armed robbers in Hackney. He was also wanted by the police there in connection with murder, rape, prostitution and dealing in crack cocaine.

Blackwood was arrested at a crack den in Dalston in 1988 and was found to be in possession of illegal drugs. Branded 'the most dangerous man in Britain', he was deported, officially for entering the country illegally. He was sent back to Jamaica where he was wanted for killing a policeman. Nevertheless, the following year, he was seen back in London, though underworld contracts were said to be out on him. In 1990, after being deported from the United States, he was arrested in Canada for allegedly slashing his girlfriend's face with a knife after entering the country illegally on a fake passport. He attempted to gain refugee status there, claiming that he feared for his life in Jamaica due to his political affiliations. In 1996, he was seen back in Birmingham. Living in a series of safe house and using six aliases, he was blamed for introducing crack to Scotland where it fetched a higher price than in English towns. He was said to have ordered the killing of 20-year-old Wolverhampton drug dealer and semi-professional footballer Kevin Nunes in 2002 for trying to muscle in on his lucrative cocaine trade in Aberdeen, Dundee and Edinburgh. Nunes had tried out for Spurs after moving to Britain from Jamaica in 1998. He was shot dead in a country lane ten miles from Wolverhampton.

'The signs are that this was an underworld hit,' a police source said.

Five gangsters involved in what turned out to be a firing squad-style execution were eventually jailed in January 2008. At the time, a wave of Yardie gun crime was sweeping across London and the Midlands. The girlfriends of two top gangsters had been working at a London police station. One of them had access to intelligence about operations against the Yardies.

Despite rumours and the occasional sighting, Blackwood's whereabouts remained unknown. This is reputed to be because of his mastery of black magic. He once survived an attack in which his nose was lopped off and his skull split open with a machete, which added to the mystique surrounding his occult beliefs. Blackwood's pal 'Yardie Ron' Rowan was not so lucky. Attacked outside an illegal drinking club, he was peppered with bullets from five different guns. Around that time, police entered a Brixton nightclub to discover that the ceiling was so full of bullet holes it was about to collapse. This was not the result of gang warfare. Visiting Yardies liked to fire a few rounds into the air to the rhythm of the bass.

When Blackwood was in North America, the Yardies came to the attention of the public in London again in October 1991 when Brixton drug dealer Mark Burnett was shot dead in full view of reggae concert-goers after he accidentally stepped on the toe of a notorious Yardie gunman at the Podium nightclub in Vauxhall, south London. Not one person out of the 2,000-strong crowd came forward to help the police with their inquiries. Some 350 claimed to have been in the toilets when the shooting took place. Detectives, who took the names of 116 potential witnesses, discovered that 90 per cent of the names and addresses they had been given were false. Of the few who did not give false names and the 270 who were arrested immediately after the incident, none could recall seeing anything out of the ordinary. After a police hotline failed to receive a single call, Burnett's family were so frustrated that they put up a £10,000 reward for anyone giving information leading to a conviction. It remained unclaimed.

The rise of the Yardies coincided with the spread of cocaine and crack. In the early 1990s, the amount of cocaine seized doubled every year. Once the drug of the rich, crack made cocaine available to the less privileged. Small-time cannabis street dealers who presented little threat of violence were soon replaced by crack dealers who were armed. For Yardies, carrying a gun is almost like wearing a fashion accessory; it went along with fast cars and pretty girls.

'It's all about building up what they call their "rep", meaning reputation as a hard man,' said Detective Superintendent John Jones. Killings were worn as a 'badge of honour' and to tell others 'they were not to be messed with'. They introduced a cycle of violence where no Yardie stayed on top for very long. This caused problems for the police. In the traditional British model of organised crime, the police would target the leader, 'Mr Big'. Once he was taken out, the gang collapsed. But with the Yardies, Mr Big was more likely to be taken out by one of his own men seeking to move up the ladder. The average life expectancy for a Yardie was about 35.

Realising that their lifespan was short, Yardies had no interest in investing or laundering money. Rather they want to show off their wealth with clothes, jewellery, cars and other forms of instant display. Yardie Michael Andrews, deported from Britain after three years of stealing and dealing crack and cocaine in Bristol and London, explained the Yardies' live-for-today philosophy. 'We grow up with nothing and when we get something we don't know how long it will last so we use it then. It also means you can lose it there and then. You can still be the big man and have lots of respect, but when the police see you standing on a corner trying to sell a rock of crack, they leave you alone. They think you're not a top player any more.'

The police made little headway against the Yardies. In March 1988, they had set up Operation Lucy but found that trying to keep up surveillance on Yardies was a daunting task. They were constantly on the move. Usually suspects had several different women and several different cars. They would leave a party in London at 3am and drive to a shebeen in Birmingham for a couple of drinks, then head back to London. The police soon found that comparisons with the Mafia or other crime gangs did not stand up. The Yardies represented not so much organised crime as 'disorganised crime'.

After four years the Metropolitan Police closed down Operation Lucy because they feared they might be accused of racism. A senior officer, fighting to keep the project alive, sent a report stating: 'What other group of people outside Northern Ireland are so well armed and go round shooting at people as a matter of routine?'

The operation was followed by Operation Dalehouse, a joint police-customs unit that concentrated on curbing the crack business in Brixton. It seized drugs with an estimated street value of £1 million and made 274 arrests, though obtained few convictions for serious crimes. Then it, too, was closed down over concerns about accusations of racism.

Next, the police tried to infiltrate the gangs. In 1991,

they thought they'd got lucky when double-dealing Yardie Eaton Green fell into their lap. Green was from Kingston, Jamaica, where he dropped out of school at the age of 12. In the run-up to the election in October 1980, the political parties had teamed up with street gangs to fight for control of the country. Green joined Michael Manley's People's National Party (PNP), who put a gun in his hand.

Green belonged to the Desert Posse who with the Kremlin Posse and the Rapid Posse made up the Max Gang. With the help of corrupt policemen and politicians, they soon amassed enough recruits and weapons to take over the Tel Aviv neighbourhood of Kingston and become the Tel Aviv Crew. They had handguns, shotguns and fully automatic M16 assault rifles; many of the guns were supplied by a senior politician in the PNP. Thus armed, they ran the all-night drinking shebeens. Anyone who got in their way was shot. Through drug trafficking they established contacts in Miami, New York and London.

In early 1991 Green was about to stand trial for shooting with intent to kill. This time he faced a long stretch in the medieval conditions of St Catherine's Prison. The witnesses showed no signs of disappearing. His bail was about to be revoked and so, on 12 February, he boarded a British Airways flight to London. Carrying a passport in his own name he landed at Gatwick Airport. Once he had cleared immigration, he hooked up with old friends from Kingston and, effectively, disappeared. He hung out in Steppers wine bar and the Fiveways Café in Brixton, and went drinking and played cards in the illegal gambling houses on Kingsland High Road in Dalston.

That May, Green was arrested in Brixton by Acting

Detective Constable Steve Barker for a minor traffic offence. The young officer found that Green was carrying an offensive weapon and persuaded him to become an informant. Green later claimed that he had done this because he was sick of being exploited by political parties and drug gangs and decided to take his revenge by betraying them. However, he had little choice. Arrested on a firearms offence, he was in imminent danger of being sent back to Jamaica.

His co-operation with the police was not a casual affair. He was a professional informant, code named Aldridge Clarke and paid up to £1,000 a time for his assistance. Over the next two years, he supplied 168 detailed intelligence reports, giving names, contact details and information about the activities of everyone he knew in London's Yardie colony. DC Barker duly passed these on to the Metropolitan Police's specialist intelligence department SO11. Extracts from reports he gave to the police that were later published paint a vivid picture of Yardie activities in London.

May 15, 1992: Two Jamaicans known as Mitch and Scott are in Dalston. They both have guns which they nearly always carry and normally rob people of drugs. Both wear rolled up woollen hats which I think are masks when they are rolled down.

July 22, 1992: Kirk and Blackbeard have just left in a cab, a black Sierra, E reg, from Shepherd's Bush to go to Brixton. Duane stayed there and they are going to pick him up. They have the Luger and the

.45 automatic. They will maybe look for him in Railton Road.

February 8, 1993: There are three Jamaicans dealing from the flats in ***** Road. There is a stairway by the church where they meet the buyers. You have to ring them on a Vodafone to arrange when to meet them. They can supply any amount of crack you want.

February 12, 1993: There is a crack house in ******* Road, E5. It is a little house along a pathway. They are dealing about five ounces a day. Tuffy and Sprat are taking it over. There are normally two or three guns inside. That is where the dealing is done. The back door is always left open for a quick escape.

May 10, 1993: Tuffy, Pekos, Eric and Troy went to a bookmakers in ****** Road and tried to get them to sell crack. The police were called and Troy hid a gun in the bin, which the police later found. There is a hidden camera at the bookies. Last week, Tuffy, Blue, Ninja and Twitch robbed a gambling house in Dalston with guns and wearing masks. During the robbery, Ninja pulled off his mask and said he is not hiding and fired three shots into the air. Some Spanglers members were at the gambling house. Tuffy forced Juggaland to get on his knees and took his jewellery.

May 10, 1993. There is a Jamaican known as Ratty now in London. He is wanted in Jamaica for murder. He is living in Brixton. Tuffy has threatened to kill Ratty because of something to do with a death in Kingston. Ratty was at Splash wine bar two days ago. He always carries a gun and has an Uzi.

June 2, 1993: A local youth tried to come into Steppers with two guns, a replica and a shotgun sawn-off. The replica was an automatic, like a Taurus. The youth tried to get in with the guns and they were taken off him.

June 11, 1993: Twitch is running with Ninja Blue and Barry Dog. They are robbing people with guns in north London.

June 23, 1993: 4.40pm, phone call. Cecil and Larry are going to the half-kilo rip-off tonight, the one that they didn't do on Monday night. The man they are going to rip off lives in Stockwell. They will be parked up somewhere in the road about 1am waiting for him, with two guns.

June 24, 1993: 1.30pm, phone call. They went to do the job last night but the boy who set it up for them called them and cancelled it about 12.30pm because it was too hot, the police were about, so the man with the half-kilo was too frightened to leave his shop all night. They say there is no rush, they can do it any time.

In his reports to Barker, Green tracked the arrival in London of one Yardie after another, as the Jamaican posses expanded their empire. 'Killer' moved to Dalston and started selling crack cocaine. 'Blackbeard' moved in with a girl called Debbie in Shepherd's Bush and started selling crack. 'Pepsi', the top man from the Rapid Posse, moved to Nottingham where he too started selling crack. Then Nookie moved in to Forest Gate where he started selling crack.

Green explained how the 'rude boys' – the ordinary members of the Yardie posses – drank all night in shebeens, and almost all of them had a handgun in their pocket.

'Everybody in London carry a gun,' he said. Sometimes, when they were feeling good, they would whip them out and fire live bullets into the ceiling; they called it, 'Saluting the music'. And they shot people in a casual, almost bored kind of way.

'Nitty Gritty was killed by Supercat ... There was a shooting at the club in Arcola Street, Stoke Newington ... Steve chased a man into Kingsland High Road and fired three shots at him ... Banbury and Pecos robbed everyone at Harry's Café with guns yesterday ... Ritchie was shot in a bar in Hackney by Thin Hand Barry...' Green reported it all.

Hardly a week passed when he did not contact Barker. They met in police stations, a Home Office building, supermarket car parks. On other occasions, Green simply phoned his latest report through. When Barker was sent to Jamaica, Green called him there on his mobile. Green's information was recorded in Registered Informant Reports at SO11 and extracts were fed to three specialist incident rooms targeting crack dealers.

Barker also patched Green through to the district attorney's office in New York. This was done so that the

District Attorney could track Tapper Zoochie's contacts with dealers in Manhattan and watch out for Puppy Dog, 'who is now out of prison and has his M16 back' and for Roamy, who had settled in 91st Street, Queens and 'has just smuggled a Taurus automatic handgun from New York to Jamaica'. As he filed each informant report, DC Barker added his own official assessment. He gave Green 'Grade A' for access and '1' for accuracy. A1 was the highest rating.

As well as pursuing a lucrative career as a stool pigeon, Green was also peddling crack cocaine to street dealers near the Fiveways Café in Brixton, on Kingsland High Road and in the crack houses in Nottingham. And he carried a gun. He was, after all, a Yardie.

Scotland Yard knew all about his involvement with cocaine and firearms. On the night of 23 November 1991 – just six months after he had become a grass – Green attended a party in Loughborough Road, Brixton, along with 300 other people who were drinking, dancing and smoking. In the midst of them, Green ran into well-known Brixton figure Stepper Dan. An argument broke out.

'Shoot me then,' one of them shouted. 'You're always saying you're gonna shoot me. Shoot me then.'

Then the firing started. The guests scattered. Stepper Dan took a bullet in the right arm, while Green was shot in the stomach. But they continued grappling. Holding onto each other, they crashed down the stairs, dropping their guns as they fell. Stepper Dan's arm was broken and Green was bleeding profusely. But no one wanted the police on the scene, so no one called an ambulance. Instead, someone fetched a VW convertible and drove them to the A&E at

King's College Hospital in Camberwell. Green's wound was so severe that he lost a kidney. And when they undressed him, hospital staff found two rocks of crack cocaine in Green's jacket pocket.

The police could hardly fail to get involved in such a serious incident. But Stepper Dan alone was charged with possession of a firearm and attempted murder. Green was placed on an ID parade, but he was not charged in connection with the shooting. Two weeks later, the charges against Stepper Dan were dropped. Green still faced prosecution over the crack cocaine, but those charges were dropped as well.

According to Home Office guidelines 'The need to protect an informant does not justify granting him immunity from arrest or prosecution.' But clearly, that was what Scotland Yard had just done. Later an enquiry criticised senior officers for keeping such an active and dangerous criminal on the Metropolitan Police's payroll.

Green was not only selling crack to street dealers. He also took the opportunity to rob some of them at gunpoint. One woman describes how she saw him put his gun in an African dealer's mouth before stealing an ounce of cocaine and a roll of cash from him. He often sat in a local gambling house with a gun in front of him, selling or stealing as the mood took him.

During his career as an informant, Green was arrested on two further occasions. On 25 August 1992, the drugs squad raided a house in Queensdale Crescent, Shepherd's Bush. Green was arrested, released on bail then informed that he faced no charge. On 13 January 1993, he was caught in another raid on a house in Loftus Road,

Shepherd's Bush. This time he was charged with possession of cocaine with intent to supply, but the case never came to trial.

Having overstayed his visitor's visa, Green should have been deported. In fact, as he had jumped bail on a serious charge in Jamaica, he should have been sent back instantly. However, the Home Office granted him permanent residence on the grounds of his marriage to a British national. Green had first applied for residence immediately after becoming an informant. Then in July 1991, when his visa was about to expire, he made a second application, saying that he was about to marry an entirely different woman named Sharon Clarke. Normally, immigration officers would have suspected that this was a marriage of convenience. However, on 21 November 1991, Sharon Clarke gave birth to a boy named Keston. Apparently, the immigration authorities accepted that he was Green's son, though Sharon Clarke was already four months pregnant before she met Green and did not name him as the boy's father on the birth certificate. The immigration officers also accepted, after 'copious checks with the police', that Green had not come to police attention while he had been in the country.

During Green's two years as an informant, a number of Yardies entered the country illegally, even though Green informed his handlers of their arrival. For example, at 9pm on 11 June 1992, Green telephoned Barker to report that the well-known Yardie, Blackbeard, who had already been deported, had just arrived illegally from Kingston. He provided the name, address and telephone number of the woman Blackbeard was staying with, along with a detailed physical description. Nevertheless, no attempt was made to arrest Blackbeard and send him back again. He was allowed to stay in the UK where, according to Green's subsequent reports, he sold crack, drove around London with a .45 automatic and a Luger, robbed another Yardie at gunpoint and, on one wild night, crashed his girlfriend's car into three parked vehicles.

Green also warned of the imminent arrival of a Kingston gunman known as Showie. He provided his real name and noted that he had already been deported. However, Showie walked through the airport unimpeded. A few weeks later he was seen at the murder scene of Christopher 'Tuffy' Bourne, the most powerful Yardie in London at the time.

In October 1992, Green reported that his friend Rohan Thomas, better known as Colonel Bumpy, was planning to come to Britain with his cohort Cecil Thomas, no relation. Over the next six months, Green filed eight different reports on Bumpy, crediting him with ten murders and warning that he was threatening to murder a witness in a forthcoming trial, whether this information was accurate or not. DC Barker was so interested that he allowed Green to telephone Bumpy in Jamaica from Thornton Heath police station. Barker planned, he said, to use the two men as 'a magnet for intelligence'. Green sent money to pay for their tickets, though Scotland Yard later denied providing it.

On 28 March, when Bumpy and Cecil arrived at Gatwick Airport, Scotland Yard, Immigration and Customs all knew all about it. Customs targeted the two men for a drugs search but found nothing. Immigration secretly filmed their arrival and covertly copied their passports. Although both men had criminal records and Bumpy was using a fake passport, they were allowed to enter the country.

On Saturday, 29 May 1993, around 150 people gathered for a blues party in a warehouse in Nottingham. At about 3.30am the following morning, five men carrying guns suddenly turned off the music. A guy with a red bandana tied around his head fired his gun into the ceiling and yelled, 'We are the SAD Squad – Seek and Destroy.'

The gang then set about systematically robbing everyone there. They took cash, credit cards, mobile phones, jewellery, even the rings off their fingers. The robbers beat up several victims. The guy with the red bandana shot one man in the leg and stood over him jeering: 'Bleed, pussy, bleed.'

The sheer brazenness of the raid and the casual violence of the robbers caused a sensation in Nottingham. Detectives in Nottingham turned to informers in the city's drugs scene for help. The robbers, they were told, were Jamaican Yardies from London. No one knew much about them except for the one with the red bandana. He was a professional gunman from Kingston who was known on the streets as 'Leon'.

When Nottingham detectives called their colleagues in London, they were passed on to a young Brixton detective who was now renowned for his knowledge of Yardies: Steve Barker. He told them that 'Leon' was Eaton Green. However, when Nottingham detectives came to London looking for him, SO11 did nothing to help.

On 19 June, nearly three weeks after the robbery, Stoke Newington police made a drugs raid on a house in Belgrade

Road, Stoke Newington. They found Bumpy Thomas sitting in bed. There was a loaded Luger hidden under the mattress. He went for it and his hand was only inches away from the gun when they grabbed him.

This was embarrassing for Scotland Yard. Letting a known criminal enter the country illegally was bad enough, but now he had tried to pull a gun on fellow officers. Nine days later, things got even worse. On 28 June Green informed his handlers: 'The gun that Bumpy got nicked with was a German Luger. That was the gun they used in a shooting in Nottingham.' He was talking about the warehouse party robbery. Scotland Yard decided not to pass on this tip to the Nottinghamshire force. If they arrested Bumpy, how he got into the country would come out in open court.

Even without the help of SO11, Nottingham detectives were close on the heels of all five men who had raided the warehouse party. By early July, they had found out for themselves that Bumpy was involved and approached the Metropolitan Police to ask them to hand him over. They had identified three other suspects – Steve Crossdale who they arrested in south London, Cecil Thomas who had come through Gatwick with Bumpy, and Errol 'Tall Larry' Lynch.

They did not know where Cecil and Tall Larry were, but Scotland Yard did. On 29 June, Green made a series of phone calls reporting every move the couple made as they set out for south London with a gun in their grey Ford Orion. Scotland Yard tracked the car through the streets using a helicopter. Then they staged an armed ambush, arresting the pair for possession of a firearm, apparently quite unaware that they were wanted in Nottingham.

Of the five men who had raided the warehouse party, only Eaton Green was still at liberty. When Nottingham officers could not find him, they turned again for help to Yardie expert DC Barker. Barker said he would help them trace Green, but he did not. Instead, at 4pm on 6 July, he phoned Green and arranged to meet him at the Home Office Immigration building in Lower Thames Street. They met at 7pm. Green named a Yardie in Nottingham who had supplied a shotgun for the warehouse robbery and two others who had bought some of the stolen jewellery. The Nottinghamshire constabulary were not informed of this meeting or given this crucial evidence against the men who were now under arrest.

Although Barker had known for five weeks that Green was wanted by Nottingham police he made no attempt to detain him, and Green walked away from the meeting a free man. Two days later, using information they had obtained from the DSS, the Nottingham officers traced Green to a girlfriend's house in east London. Just before 2pm on Thursday, 8 July 1993, the group of detective surrounded a slim young black man with a scar across his right cheek as he walked down Mandela Road in Newham. They handcuffed Green and told him that they were arresting him for possession of firearms and conspiracy to rob.

That afternoon, they headed back up the M1 with their suspect. With them, they had their intelligence profile of their captive.

Name: Eaton Leonard Green, known as 'Leon'
Born: 21 September 1967 in Kingston, Jamaica

Age: 27

Address: various flats in London since February 1991

They also knew that he was a Yardie and that he was their chief suspect in the Nottingham warehouse party robbery. What they did not know was that Eaton Green was a Scotland Yard informant – not some casual squealer who occasionally traded information to buy his way out of trouble but a full-time, registered intelligence asset with his own codename, a top secret file, two specialist handlers and a two-year history of supplying high-grade intelligence on the Yardies to the Metropolitan Police, the Home Office, Customs and Excise, the Jamaican government and the New York District Attorney. Eaton Green was SO11's secret weapon in the war against organised crime.

Green was not about to tell the Nottingham police any of this. If it came out that he had grassed up some of the Yardies' top men, his life would be in danger. However, Scotland Yard had a problem. Under the Home Office guidelines, it was 'a prime consideration' that 'police must never commit themselves to a course which, whether to protect an informant or otherwise, will constrain them to mislead a court'. In these circumstances, Scotland Yard should have gone to the Crown Prosecution Service at the earliest possible opportunity and explained the situation. They did not. Instead, Scotland Yard kept the Nottingham police and the CPS in the dark.

As the time for the trial approached, SO11 sent the judge a secret 'mitigation text'. This was a device used by Scotland Yard to reduce an informant's sentence without blowing his cover in open court. However, four weeks into the trial, two defence lawyers went to the judge in chambers and said they suspected their clients to have been betrayed by an informer. The judge knew from the mitigation text that this was true. Fearing that their top informant was about to be unmasked, SO11 tried to get the prosecution to drop the case – even though that meant allowing five armed robbers to go free. A senior officer from Scotland Yard even called the judge. Nevertheless, the judge and the prosecution stuck to their guns and told the defence that Green had betrayed their clients. Green was whisked from the court and held under armed guard.

The defence lawyers then asked to see his informer's file. To prevent this, Scotland Yard continued to try to abort the trial, but the Attorney General and the Director of Public Prosecutions ruled against them. But when the file turned up in court, 86 of the 168 reports Green had made were missing. There was not a single report between 24 May 1991, when Green first met Barker, and 15 May 1992. There was no reference, for example, to the shooting incident with Stepper Dan. Scotland Yard maintained that these documents had been shredded in a routine clearout of the files – though they were barely a year old and concerned criminals who were still active on the streets of London.

The judge then weeded out any material he considered irrelevant to the case. Among the remaining material were the two reports from Green that referred to the Nottingham robbery. These disclosed that the gun under Bumpy's mattress had been used at the robbery and named the two people who had bought stolen jewellery. At the bottom of these two informant reports was written

'Liaising with Nottingham' and 'Direct to Nottingham'. However, this information was never received.

The wrangling between the Nottinghamshire police, Scotland Yard, the CPS and the DPP took so long that the judge stopped the trial. With his cover blown, Green admitted his guilt in the warehouse robbery and made a statement to Nottingham detectives. At a new trial with a new jury seven months later, Eaton Green was the Crown's lead witness.

Rohan 'Bumpy' Thomas was jailed for 14 years. Steve Crossdale got eight. Cecil Thomas and Tall Larry were acquitted but deported back to Jamaica. However, the Court of Appeal quashed the convictions obtained on Green's testimony. Nevertheless, Bumpy Thomas's convictions on two other firearms charges stood and he was deported.

Green was given a reduced sentence of six years, served under special protection. Even though he was held in the Protective Witness Unit at Parkhurst, where 12 supergrasses were held in isolation, Green did not feel safe from the Yardie drug barons who had targeted him for revenge. In 1997, he grabbed a kitchen knife and slashed a prisoner known as Ali, who lost so much blood he was inches away from death; Ali needed 19 stitches in his head.

At the end of his sentence, Green remained in Parkhurst for his own protection, though Nottingham police had served a deportation order on him. After a two-year legal battle, Green gave up his attempt to claim political asylum, on the grounds that his life would have been in danger if he'd been sent back to Jamaica.

'He's dead,' said a former friend. 'He'll never get off the plane.'

The Yardies hit the headlines with the murder of a policeman in 1993. On 20 October, 31-year-old father-of-five William 'Kwame' Danso was watching a football match with a friend at Cato Road, Clapham. Shortly after 9pm Danso answered his front door. Three black men armed with a baseball bat and two handguns fired a total of 12 shots at him. He was hit six times and died.

Local Clapham community officer, 45-year-old PC Patrick Dunne, was attending an incident in a house across the street when he heard the sound of gunfire. Dunne went outside to investigate, followed by the householder and a friend. A gun was brandished and the policeman shouted at the two others: 'Get in! Get in!'

There was a shot. A single bullet pierced his hand and chest, killing him. Witnesses heard the gang laughing as they walked off, firing triumphant shots into the air. Neither Danso nor Dunne had been armed and these victims had not presented any sort of danger to the gunmen.

Three men – including 23-year-old Yardie gang leader Gary Nelson, said by the police to be 'one of the most violent and dangerous men to walk the streets of Britain' – were charged with the murder in November 1993. Nelson had been arrested, along with Richard Watts and Tony Francis, after they opened fire on an unmarked police car that had been tailing them. During questioning at Islington police station Nelson was filmed saying, 'Watch yourself Sergeant, watch yourself Mr Sergeant, watch yourself.' Then he stood up and said: 'You'll cop it like the other fucker copped it.' Nevertheless, the murder case was dropped due to insufficient evidence.

After the shooting of Danso and Dunne, Nelson had

gone to Jamaica. When he returned in 1994 he was jailed for the shooting, which he claimed was a road rage incident. He was released in 1999. Then the Dunne-Danso case was reopened in 2001, partly due to pressure from the victims' families. After a televised appeal on *Crimestoppers*, a prisoner at Wormwood Scrubs told police Nelson bragged in jail that he had 'shot the copper – the one on the bike'. Dunne was known as the 'cycling cop' in that area of Clapham.

An all-forces bulletin was put out, saying that, as well as being a suspect in the murder of PC Dunne, Nelson had also been 'found not guilty of the attempted murder of two north London police officers and two further attempted murders, one of which is believed to be drug related. His custodial behaviour has been consistently disruptive and he is suspected of involvement in the prison drug scene and bullying. He has also assaulted and made serious threats against staff.'

According to the police, he was a fitness fanatic and womaniser whose mobile phone voicemail said: 'I'm too sexy for my phone.' He spent his cash on Prada clothes, Louis Vuitton luggage and heavy gold jewellery and, at the time of his arrest, was planning to buy an Aston Martin sports car.

On top of that he was a drug dealer, extortionist and gangland enforcer who had so many enemies he sometimes slept in body armour. Since the age of 15 he had been convicted of 21 offences, including robbery, theft, assault and possession of firearms. He was cleared of the attempted murder of a bouncer who had been shot outside a nightclub in Victoria in 1993. Police sources said

Nelson's motto was simply: 'The gun is might and might is right.' He called his Browning pistol 'my special thing'.

'Nelson is a major league, organised criminal who will use extreme violence in pursuit of his aims,' said Detective Chief Inspector Steve Richardson. 'He is a wealthy man, not only from dishonesty but legitimate operations funded by his ill-gotten gains. He is also extremely clever. He is undoubtedly one of the most dangerous men in the country … He is not just a hit man, he is at the top. He is notorious in south London.'

But there was a problem bringing him to justice for the Danso and Dunne murders.

'Many people fear him,' said DCI Richardson, 'and a number of potential witnesses refused to give statements.'

Nelson – also known as 'Tyson' – boasted in one of his trials: 'I walk heavy. I am a serious person.'

Eventually the police bugged his flat in London's Dockland. In November 2004, they raided the apartment to find him watching a pornographic film and he was arrested for murder. Searching his house, they found a 'hit-man's kit' in a small zip-up bag. It included a Browning semi-automatic pistol, a silencer and a laser sight. This alone was enough to earn him a life sentence.

Finally, in February 2006, Nelson was convicted of the double murder. During the month-long trial, the jury were protected and armed police patrolled outside the court. Nelson himself refused to attend the hearing at Woolwich Crown Court, opting to stay in his cell at Belmarsh Prison.

The court heard that Ghanaian-born William Danso had been a bouncer at the Brixton Academy and had refused Nelson entry. He also worked as a security guard in Street

Communications, a mobile-phone shop in Leigham Court Road, Streatham. At about 5pm on the night on the shooting, he had intervened in an argument between Tony Francis, a friend of Nelson's, and a man named 'Blue'. Detectives travelled to Ghana and tracked down Eugene Djaba, the manager of the shop where Danso had been working. Djaba had fled after jumping bail in 1996 and was convicted in his absence of a £3-million cigarette fraud. Consequently, he was reluctant to return to Britain. In a highly unusual move, he was allowed to testify via video link. He said that he had seen Nelson pull a gun from his jacket the day before the murders and threaten to put a 'bullet in the belly' of another man. The weapon was later identified as an Italian-made Tanfoglio pistol.

Danso had 'acted calmly and professionally in defusing the situation with the minimum of fuss,' the court was told. 'But Nelson and his friends, applying some utterly warped sense of values and of their own importance, decided that for these acts of so-called disrespect William Danso had to die.'

They armed themselves with two handguns and a baseball bat. Then the three of them sought Danso out at his home and killed him, even though he was unarmed and defenceless. Across the road PC Dunne was also 'unarmed and of no immediate threat to Nelson,' the judge said. 'Nonetheless, Nelson had decided that he, too, had to die.'

Outside Danso's house in Cato Road 13 cartridge cases and nine bullets had been found. They had been fired by a Browning 9mm pistol and a Tanfoglio 9mm. Mobile-phone evidence showed that a phone linked to Nelson was in the Cato Road area at the time of the murder and stopped being used almost immediately afterwards. A witness had seen a vehicle with a partial number plate '8 MOB' or '9 MOB' in the area at the time of the murder. Another witness had seen Nelson driving a black BMW 3 series with the number plate A9 MOB on 2 November 1993, two weeks after the murders. He was later arrested on 23 November 1993 in Highbury in possession of a firearm while driving this car.

On 6 June 1994, acting on information received through an earlier episode of *Crimestoppers*, police found a tin at Wandsworth Cemetery containing two 'Bally' bags and a Virgin Airlines bag as well as a disassembled Browning 9mm and Tanfoglio 9mm. The guns were shown by forensic analysis to be those used in the murders. A fingerprint on one of the bags was identified as that of Nelson's mother and the Virgin bag identified as one given to passengers on flights including those made by Nelson's mother between Gatwick and Miami on 10 September and 24 September 1993.

Nelson was given two life sentences with the recommendation that he serve a minimum of 35 years. Even in prison he was dangerous.

SO11 scored another own goal in 1996 when 35-year-old Delroy 'Epsi' Denton was jailed for life for the murder of 24-year-old Marcia Lawes. In Kingston, Denton had been the founder of the Rapid Posse and had taken part in the murderous gang wars. He had served time in Jamaica for armed robbery and firearms offences. He was known to be extremely dangerous, having used an ice pick to murder a prostitute. In 1993, he entered the UK on his brother's passport and signed on for social security under a false name.

On 12 May 1994, just 17 days after Denton had arrived in England, the police made a drugs raid at the Atlantic pub in Brixton. Immigration enforcement officer Brian Fotheringham was on hand looking for illegal immigrants. He became suspicious of a slim young Jamaican who had been found in possession of a knife. He said he was a British national called Clive Lloyd Johnson, but Fotheringham had come across that name before, when it was being used falsely by other Yardies. Fotheringham advised the police not to release the suspect on bail and set about tracing the real Clive Johnson.

The following day, Fotheringham returned to the police station to interview the impostor, who offered two further false identities before finally admitting that his real name was Delroy Denton and immediately asking for political asylum. His life, he said, was in danger from corrupt politicians in Jamaica.

Fotheringham had seen Denton's name in police intelligence reports. Warrants for his arrest for the murder of seven women had been issued in his native Jamaica. Fotheringham wrote in the interview notes: 'We need long-term detention (secure) on this one.' On the standard form requesting detention, he wrote: 'Subject dangerous Jamaican criminal, given 16 years in Jamaica for firearms/aggravated burglary offences. Entered on false ID. Has been claiming in yet another false ID. Very dangerous individual.' He then completed a special Exceptional Risk Form to warn the Metropolitan Police of the presence in London of this unusually dangerous man. On this form, Fotheringham ticked two boxes positioned alongside the statements 'He is associated with a dangerous gang' and

'He is of an extremely violent nature'. Fotheringham knew that Denton might buy himself a short stay in Britain with an asylum application; he wanted to ensure that he spent it behind bars.

The next day, following a conversation with SO11, Fotheringham wrote a new file note. It said that there was 'no realistic chance of long-term detention on this man' as 'PC Barker has stated intelligence has shown that subject has not been involved in any serious criminal matters since being here'. Denton had agreed to become an informer. He was allowed to walk out on to the streets of London and given £50 a week by the Home Office; he continued signing on. Four months later, Denton's asylum application was rejected. However, he was not deported. The memo requesting his removal simply stayed in the file.

On 19 December 1994, a south-London woman called the local police to report that her daughter had been raped. The girl alleged that she and three friends used to laugh with a man they sometimes saw at the bus stop on their way home from school. One day, they had decided to skip school and go round to his flat. After they had drunk some wine and smoked a joint, her daughter had fallen asleep. Her friends left and when she woke up she alleged that she found the man forcing himself on her. She maintained that she had struggled and pleaded but he did not stop. His name was Delroy Denton.

The police went to his home, Denton fled, but he was caught and charged with rape. After six weeks in custody, he was released when the CPS dropped the rape charge on grounds of insufficient evidence. Neither would they prosecute him for having sex with an underage girl because, it turned out, she was not a virgin and consequently could not be said to have been 'corrupted'. Denton was back out on the streets of London.

Scotland Yard had bought him a mobile phone so he could report in and he spent the money the Home Office had given him on dope and crack. Every so often, he contacted Steve Barker with information about his acquaintances. However, none of the crimes he reported were as heinous as the one he was about to commit.

Marcia Lawes lived in a small flat in a quiet street on the edge of Brixton in south London with her two-year-old son, Cassius, and her baby daughter, Malika. She was unemployed and had split from the father of her children. In the past she had suffered from a crippling depression but had stayed in touch with her family, particularly with her elder sister, Mercy, and was beginning to make a life for herself.

On 18 April 1995, Marcia had left her children with the child minder down the street and was alone in the flat when Denton rang the doorbell and talked his way in. He raped her, stabbed her 18 times around the chest, neck and shoulders, and left her lying dead on the floor of her hallway.

When no one had seen Marcia for three days, Mercy began to worry. Around half-past-seven in the evening, she went round to the flat with some friends. They forced open the front door to find Marcia lying sprawled across the hall carpet on her back with multiple stab wounds to her chest and throat. Her clothes were dishevelled and it was clear that she had been the victim of some kind of sexual attack.

Detectives from the Number Five Area Major

Investigation Pool were called in. They quickly ruled out any of Marcia's male friends, using the DNA from the semen on her body. On 9 May, they questioned Denton. He was arrested on 28 June and charged with murder. The CPS later dropped the charge on the grounds that there was insufficient evidence. PC Barker continued to use him as a source of intelligence.

However, the detectives were gradually rebuilding their case. On 23 December 1995, they arrested Denton again and, in July 1996, he was jailed for life for rape and murder.

From prison, Denton wrote to a penpal explaining the dangerous psychology of the Yardies.

'To get recognition in a gang you have to do things to attract attention from the leader,' he said. 'It's a question of kill or be killed. By 1980, Jamaica was on fire. I started to do a lot of things and was out of control. Things went from bad to worse. It was a day and night thing. I started to kill seriously.'

By 1998, the Metropolitan Police had set up Operation Trident to counter 'black-on-black' killings. In May 1999, 28-year-old Laverne Forbes and her partner 31-year-old Patrick Smith were shot in the head in their north London flat. Their seven-year-old daughter witnessed both killings. Then on 14 June, 51-year-old sound engineer Henry Lawes was gunned down by a gang of five men outside his home in Harlesden, north-west London. Once he was on the ground, his killers ruthlessly finished him off.

In July 1999, a rally was held in Brixton to protest about the killings. In the first six months of the year, 13 people had been killed in feuds thought to involve the Yardies. However, the shooting of white rap-DJ Tim Westwood received more media attention. He had been playing at the Lambeth Country Show in Brockwell Park and was on his way home when a gunman on a motorcycle opened fire on his car. He was hit in the right arm and his assistant, Ross Newman, received a wound to the leg. The police thought he had been the victim of a Yardie turf war.

In February 2000, four Yardies were jailed for life for a shoot-out at Bridge Park leisure centre that the prosecution said was 'more reminiscent of the Wild West than north London on a Saturday afternoon'. The Old Bailey was told that the Lock City Crew had turned the centre into their headquarters, keeping arms, ammunition and drugs there. On 1 May 1999, 29-year-old Dion Holmes was shot through the heart at close range.

'He was shot by one of the armed gang who descended on the sports complex on a mission of revenge and retribution,' said the prosecutor Richard Howell. 'Their desire for revenge was based on what appears to be, of all things, a parking incident earlier that day.'

A woman had parked outside the entrance of the complex and not in a parking bay. When she was asked to park properly by a gang member, an argument ensued. The woman returned later with her husband, a member of the Cartel Crew, and insults and abuse were exchanged. When some members of the Lock City Crew arrived at the complex and discovered what had happened 'on their territory' they 'became excitable'. They believed it showed 'a certain lack of respect'.

The gang had at their disposal a variety of weapons from handguns to a sawn-off pump-action shotgun. Carrying the guns in a sports bag, they locked the doors to prevent people from leaving before letting off shots from the sawn-off shotgun and a handgun.

The four men convicted denied murder. They were 22-year-old Jermaine 'My Lord' Hamilton, of Kilburn, west London, who had been cleared at the Old Bailey in 1998 of trying to murder two police constables with an automatic pistol; 27-year-old Leonard Cole of Finsbury Park, north London, and 26-year-old Stephen 'Beamer' Murray, of Kensal Green, north-west London, who had both stayed in Britain after their six-month tourist visas expired; and 38-year-old Winston 'Escobar' Harris, also of Kensal Green, who got into Britain on a false passport and was wanted in New York State for a drugs-related murder.

The area around Dalston, where 'Rankin' Dread' was first caught, continued to be a centre for Yardie activities. There were six gangland-style executions in the area around Lower and Upper Clapton Roads between 1999 and 2001. At the time, the sound of gunshots was more common in Dalston than any other part of Britain. There were also numerous other woundings and countless occasions when weapons had been produced and fired.

On 21 August 1999, a 38-year-old black man was shot in nearby Powell Road minutes after leaving the Chimes club. Four men were seen fleeing from another who was chasing them and firing a handgun.

On 27 March 2000, a man tried to use a stolen credit card at the Shell station on Lower Clapton road. When staff refused to return it to him, he left, returning moments later with a handgun. He began firing in a frenzy and the staff were only saved by the bulletproof glass that deflected his shots.

On 25 May 2000, 37-year-old Memet Adiguzel, a Turk, was shot six times as he sat in his car at the junction of Upper Clapton Road and Lea Bridge Road. Although it was 4.45pm, it was broad daylight and there was a host of witnesses on the street, but this did not deter the killers. Several men were arrested for the incident, which was believed to be drug-related. One of them skipped bail.

On 20 June, a man bedecked in jewellery was loitering outside a West Indian café called Too Sweet on the nearby Chatsworth Road, a short walk from Lower Clapton Road. Another man in an Afro wig walked up and shot him several times, but the victim survived.

Five days later, Meneliek Robinson was driving his red BMW convertible along Upper Clapton Road when two motorbikes, each carrying two black men, drove up behind his car. One overtook and screeched to a halt in front of him, blocking his way. The other stopped alongside. The passenger dismounted, walked up to Robinson's side window and fired several shots. Then the two motorbikes sped away. Robinson staggered from the car and collapsed on the street, where he died of massive blood loss.

The following week, 46-year-old John Nugent died after being attacked at 11pm, on the corner of Erswick Street and Lower Clapton Road. A gang of men beat him unconscious, then pushed him under a bus. He was pronounced dead on arrival at Homerton Hospital.

At 8.30pm on 23 October, a man in his early twenties was gunned down as he walked along Fountayne Road in Stoke Newington, a quarter of a mile from Lower Clapton Road. Then on 24 November, an 18-year-old boy was shot in the leg and hand on Newick Road at 11.50pm. He survived.

On 16 December 2000, 25-year-old Anthony Rose-Windon was gunned down outside Chimes. The police said he crawled to Kenning Hall Road, a few hundred yards away, where he was found dead from multiple gunshot wounds to the chest. And at 5am on 22 April 2001, the driver and passenger of a BMW were killed as they drove down Lower Clapton Road. Gunshots punched fist-sized holes in the side of the car, which then hit a Nissan Micra before coming to rest against the side of a night bus.

By 2002, Jamaican newspaper *The Gleaner* was reporting that there were 500 suspected Jamaican criminals operating in Britain, running a drugs trade that brought about 200 pounds of cocaine from Jamaica into Britain each week with a street value of more than £4.5 million. Over the previous 18 months, the traffic had increased sharply, largely as a result of tougher immigration controls by the United States. Yardie gangsters found it not only easier to enter Britain, but could also make bigger profits than in the US, where the street price of cocaine had slumped.

Jamaican gangs got cocaine from the cartels in Colombia. It was brought across the Caribbean in fast boats, which could outrun the Jamaican customs' cutters. Drug 'mules', often prostitutes working their passage, were paid £1,000 for swallowing a pound wrapped in condoms or in pellet form, before boarding a plane to London. Customs officials at Heathrow and Gatwick said they suspected that at least one in ten passengers from Jamaica were drug mules.

In January 2002, incidents involving Yardie-style gangs in London more than doubled compared to the same month the previous year. By then, the Yardies were so engrained in London that part of Brixton had become known as Little Tivoli, named after the Tivoli Gardens area of Kingston.

The police estimated there were 30 Yardie gangs operating in Britain. Some, like the Black Roses, had been smashed in Jamaica but still operated in Bristol and Brixton. One of the most powerful was known as the President's Click, an offshoot of Jamaica's notorious Shower Posse.

The Yardies had spread well outside the capital. Seven police forces covering cities including Leeds, Leicester, Southampton and Plymouth had launched operations similar to the Metropolitan police's Operation Trident. In 2001, Operation Stirrup in Leeds led to 160 arrests and 57 people being deported to Jamaica. It was followed by Operation Safeguard, which led to 30 more arrests and two more deportations in a six-day clampdown earlier in January 2002.

The Yardies often used false passports. A British 'red book' cost £150 in Jamaica. Some paid £10,000 for a marriage of convenience to a British girl. Others enrolled at bogus colleges so that their six-month tourist visas could be extended to a two-year student visa. There were thought to be 400 such colleges in Britain.

In 2002, six men from Jamaica's most-wanted list were believed to be living in Britain. They included Donovan 'Bulbie' Bennett, head of a drug-trafficking gang called Clans Massive based in Spanish Town, west of Kingston, who was thought to be personally responsible for at least 20 murders. On his return to Jamaica, he was killed at his home in Clarendon in a shoot-out with the police who wanted to question him about his involvement in 80 unsolved murders. At the time of his death, he was estimated to be worth $100 billion. Followers reacted by setting up roadblocks, shooting at the Spanish Town police station and burning effigies of National Security Minister Dr Peter Phillips.

Mark Bromley, alias 'Shotty Mark', a member of the President's Click, was in Brixton in 2004. He was wanted for a murder in April 1998, escaping from police custody and other crimes committed in Tivoli Gardens and West Kingston.

Scar-faced Glenford 'Gee' Spencer from St Catherine was number five on the most-wanted list in 2001 and was seen in Bristol the following year. Daniel Lowe was also on the run in the UK. Nicknamed 'Gun Power', he was wanted for shooting dead a 17-year-old boy who argued with him.

While the political situation in Jamaica has improved, Yardies are still active all over Britain. In July 2009, Tayside Police made a record haul of crack cocaine. In August two teenagers in Nottingham were jailed for more than nine years after burgling over 50 houses and robbing a bookmaker when the Yardies had threatened them after they lost £10,000 in a cannabis deal.

CHAPTER 6
THE AGGI CREW

The Aggi Crew, based in the St Paul's district of Bristol, take their name from the initials of surnames of the original members of the gang. They were born in the city and came to dominate Bristol's drug trade until six gang members were jailed in 1998 after being caught with more than one million pounds' worth of crack cocaine. While they were in jail, the Yardie Hype Crew and Mountain View Posse took over. But then in January 2003, several key members of the Aggi Crew were released on probation and they were determined to reclaim their old territory.

They were lucky, as a deadly rivalry had sprung up between various Yardie factions. On 10 June 2001, 18-year-old Christopher Hewitt was in the Jolly Roger pub on All Hallows Road. He had only been in Bristol a few weeks. A gang of men turned up outside carrying knifes. They sent a message into the pub – 'Tell Chrissie to come outside.' When he did, he was slashed 24 times. His stomach was ripped open and he was stabbed through the skull. A group of 15 people sat on the wall just yards away. They said they saw nothing.

The police arrested some 19 men including a former police officer. Most of them were Yardies from East Kingston, Jamaica, the original home of the Hype Crew, the Mountain View Posse, the Back to Back Gang and of most of the other Yardie gangsters that had moved into that part of Bristol. The police found no evidence against the men that they had arrested and they were released without charge.

Meanwhile, crime in the St Paul's area soared. By the end of the year, what the police defined as 'major and serious' crime had shot up by 72 per cent. And the ordinary everyday crime had shot up with it. Robberies nearly doubled that year. People breaking into cars, forcing their way into houses, snatching bags in the street. Law and order was breaking down.

That summer, the St Paul's carnival turned into a shooting match. The Burger Bar Boys came down from Birmingham. A Bristol Yardie shot one of them with a nail gun. The Burger Bar Boys pulled out their guns. The Bristol Yardies got out theirs; one of them had a machete. That night, there were at least five separate gun attacks. Nobody really knew what it was about. It might have been a squabble about a drugs deal. It might have been the backwash from some turf war over in Kingston where the Yardie gangs had their roots.

However, the police had anticipated the trouble. As early as February 2001, they had set up a special team to gather intelligence. They found there were some 200 Yardies in St

Paul's. Some of them were well-known killers in East Kingston. Within a week of Hewitt's murder, they assigned an extra 19 officers to clean up the open drugs market which was then booming around Grosvenor Road, and to target the Yardies who were behind it. They had been giving away crack cocaine and selling 'snowballs' of heroin and crack combined to expand their client base. And their success meant that on Grosvenor Road the dealers had started wearing bulletproof vests.

That autumn, the police had some success. They discovered that a local guy was running a phoney college on Lower Ashley Road, selling enrolment to nonexistent courses so that gangsters and their smugglers could slide through immigration controls, 300 of them in less than a year. In 2002, the college was busted. Forty-five of its 'students' were charged with drug offences, eleven with weapons charges, one with rape and another with attempted murder. A further 121 were detained on immigration offences while 148 went on the run.

The police set up a new unit to track the Yardies' money. They busted a greengrocer and a travel agent for money-laundering and followed streams of cash from Bristol back to Kingston. In their first year, they traced just under £10 million, some of it funding new consignments of cocaine coming to the UK, some of it buying property in Jamaica.

Then in January 2003, the police instigated Operation Atrium, a crackdown on the city's crack dealers. Around 700 were arrested; 56 were busted – 36 of them Jamaicans. However, Operation Atrium pulled in officers from all over Avon and Somerset, which meant all the divisional commanders lost men and women. They pleaded for replacements and eventually the local police authority agreed to replace the lost manpower. It would take 18 months to fund, hire and train the new officers. The street dealers they were arresting were being replaced in less than 24 hours. The police were fighting a losing battle.

Each day began with dozens of reported crimes and ended with most of them unsolved. The police would arrest people; the courts would give them bail. They would deport people. Immigration officials at the airports would let them straight back in. One of the Yardies they arrested for the murder of Christopher was known as Mr C. He was in the UK illegally, so they deported him. He came back. The police caught him again a few months later and deported him again. In October 2002, they caught him a third time and deported him yet again. This time, he was slower to return. He was shot by another gangster in Kingston.

Meanwhile the Yardies were expanding their operations and, by dealing crack and heroin, they were creating more users, who committed more crime to support their habits. Even when the courts did lock someone up it did not solve the problem; it only created a breathing space. Prolific offenders came straight back out and returned to a life of crime. The city-centre car parks noticed a surge in break-ins, simply because one local lad had been released from prison and had gone straight back to the life he knew best. This was the world the Aggi Crew returned to when they were released.

They were not on the streets long before they were ready to go to work again. Five of them put on balaclavas, picked up guns and made a tour of the local bars – the Black

Swan, the Caribbean Club, Lebeqs and the Malcolm X Centre – and announced that they were taking over. They offered the Yardies a deal, at gunpoint. They could stay and work in St Paul's, but they would have to pay for the privilege. The Aggi tax was £50 a day for each Yardie and £100 a day for any business – such as an illegal gambling den or brothel – they were running.

The Yardies were not happy about handing over their money to some local boys, so they met in a gambling den at the back of a local café to discuss the matter. And they were serious. They were, of course, armed – carrying Mag 9 automatic pistols and Brocock Magnum air pistols converted to fire live rounds. First, they agreed that they would not pay the tax. Second, they were going to take on the Aggis.

However, one of the Yardies took the Aggis' money and changed sides. The next night, in Badminton Road, one of his former mates caught up with him and shot him through the back of the knee with a 9mm handgun. It was time for the Aggi Crew to strike back. Their main man returned to the Caribbean Club, where he repeated their demands and started jeering at a bunch of Yardies. He even attacked one of them, a man called Dufus, hitting him across the face with his pistol. This was not something that a self-respecting Yardie could take lying down. Dufus went home and got his gun, came back and shot the Aggi – though he did not kill him.

In response, the Aggis attacked the Yardies' street-dealing operations. They held up the dealers at gunpoint and stole their drugs. To make their point, they drove around to a Yardie's house, dragged him out and locked him in the boot of their car. Then they drove him somewhere quiet where they pistol-whipped him. But tit-for-tat violence was not enough for the Aggi Crew. They then stormed the Black and White café on Grosvenor Road. The Black and White was legendary and had been a thorn in the side of the authorities ever since it was set up as an illegal drinking hangout in the 1970s. In 1980 it shot to national prominence when a detective constable emerging from the café with a bag of cannabis was confronted by a group of black youths, sparking one of the most serious riots in Britain since World War II. Then in the 1990s, when crack cocaine began taking over, it became the home of the Yardies. It was open 24 hours a day, seven days a week. People came from all over the West Country and South Wales to buy drugs there. It was even well known in Jamaica.

Over the years, the police have made hundreds of arrests either inside or just outside the café for offences ranging from drug dealing to robbery and assault. Drugs have been found in customers' jackets, behind a false ceiling panel, in the lavatories, in the pool tables and in the backs of speakers. Officers have been attacked by customers, and rioting broke out on two occasions in the 1980s. Weapons and illegal immigrants as well as drugs have frequently been seized at the café (which served Caribbean food, such as goat curry, along with Red Stripe beer) and several people have also reported being assaulted or held 'hostage' there.

In 2003, to make their point, two Aggis walked into the Black and White café and robbed every Yardie in there at gunpoint. Then the Aggi Crew occupied the roof of the council flats across the road from the Black and White and aimed giant fireworks like mortar rounds at the café door to oust the Yardies.

The accumulation of these incidents led the authorities to believe that a full-scale turf war was about to break out.

'Over the last few days we have seen an increase in tension between rival drug dealers,' said Chief Superintendent Mike Roe. 'Of particular concern is intelligence that these rival dealers may be prepared to use firearms against each other.'

The police saw no alternative but to put armed officers on the streets. They were fully aware that many of the Yardies had killed before, some of them many times in the internecine wars in Jamaica. Some law-abiding citizens feared that they might spark riots like those in 1980 and 1986, but the Deputy Lord Lieutenant of Bristol, David John, sought to calm public anxiety.

'The mood has changed since the eighties, when there was a feeling the police were occupying areas like St Paul's,' he said. 'Now local residents want to help the police and they want the drug dealers and people who are armed to be disarmed and locked up.'

In January 2003, for the first time in Bristol, the police would carry arms openly on the streets – not covertly in unmarked cars. The idea was to let the ordinary people of St Paul's see they were getting protection and for the gangsters to see the threat they were up against. The top priority for the police was community reassurance and public safety. Next they wanted to take the firearms off the streets and apprehend the drug dealers.

Alongside the men on the streets, the police set up a

special intelligence cell to check car numbers and IDs, and a 24-hour charging unit which would handle the paperwork generated by arrests. The armed patrols were shown mugshots of the Aggis and warned to look out for the mixed-race male with the burgundy scarf who had shot and pistol-whipped a man five days earlier. He had a silver revolver, while his accomplice was carrying a seven-inch knife. Officers were told not to use their radios as the criminals had scanners that could intercept their signals. All communication was to be via mobile phone. For their own safety, they were also told not to 'self-deploy'. Given the gangsters they were up against, they were to take co-ordinated action.

Even an armed police presence on the streets of St Paul's did not deter the criminals there. One man had his car stolen at gunpoint on Foster Street. On Denbigh Street gangsters stabbed a man before robbing him outside the St Nicholas pub where somebody left a fistful of shotgun cartridges on the bar. Even the police vans came under fire from the Aggis' fireworks at close range.

The police began to use minor offences and intelligence to revoke the parole licences of the leading Aggis and put them back behind bars. Meanwhile, on 19 June 2004, the police raided the Black and White café and seized ten wraps of crack cocaine along with small amounts of heroin and cannabis. They then used legal action under the new antisocial behaviour laws to close the place down.

Steven Wilks, the owner of the café, who took it over from his father who set it up in 1971, told a court hearing: 'For 30 years we have provided black food for the black community. I don't sell drugs. The café has been subject to negative press since day one, but closing the café is not going to change the drug situation in St Paul's. St Paul's is rife with drugs. Crack cocaine has mashed up the community and we have all felt that, myself included.'

Nevertheless, on 25 June he locked the doors and handed the keys over to the police. A few months later, the council demolished the building and the Victorian terrace it stood in to make way for social housing, an act which changed the nature of the area.

By 2007, the Aggi Crew were out of prison again, the *Economist* reported, 'but seem to have hung up their weapons'. 'The old gangs are less active now,' said Inspector Dave Bradnock.

CHAPTER 7

THE BURGER
BAR BOYS

In November 2009 a group calling themselves the Bang Bang Taliban posted rap videos celebrating gang life in Birmingham on YouTube. The rappers boasted about shooting rivals, using knives on other gang members and carrying out armed robberies. The youngsters toted guns and boasted about becoming suicide bombers. They told community workers they wanted to dominate the city's gangland – and that they would gladly be 'martyred' as Islamist terrorists. Mainly Asians from the Handsworth and Smethwick areas, they were affiliated to the notorious Burger Bar Boys. According to one community worker, nine out of ten of them had started as couriers and runners for the parent gang, but it was 'a real shock to hear them talking about suicide bombings and grinning about it.'

Under the Bang Bang Taliban video, Handsworth cops wrote: 'Birmingham Reducing Gang Related Violence has spearheaded the work dealing with the issues surrounding gangs in Birmingham, with the aim of reducing gang-related violence. Stop the guns, call Crimestoppers on 0800 555 111.' The police posted similar messages under other gang videos where youths brandished shotguns, but it seems to have done little good. In one, two masked men pointed a double-barrelled shotgun at the camera and threatened: 'I'll blow your face off.'

These new young splinter gangs identified themselves by their postcode areas and affiliated themselves with the old rivals, the Johnson Crew and Burger Bar Boys. The B21 Bang Bang youths, who recorded the shotgun-waving video, were linked to the Burgers and have posted a number of raps about shooting rival gang members. In one, a masked gangster gesturing with what appears to be a handgun tells viewers: 'Welcome to Handsworth, you're in the slum, you're in the fucking hood.' Then he tells gang members to put a 'bullet in the head' of their rivals. His partner tells the camera that 'hits' can be carried out on the cheap, warning, 'Bodies are less than £20 around here, killing is nothing.' Another rapper bragged about shooting rivals while they sleep, and silencing enemies with a shotgun. They refer to Birmingham as Baghdad, a nickname given to the city by London gangsters, while others threaten their rivals in the B6 Slash gang, which is closely tied to the Johnson Crew based in Aston and Lozells in Birmingham. The B6 Slash responded by posting their own videos, including one where they act out a 'car jacking' by hauling a rival from his car and stealing his drugs.

The rivalry between the Burger Bar Boys and the Johnson Crew made the national headlines in 2003 when 17-year-old Letisha Shakespeare and 18-year-old Charlene

Ellis were shot dead in a drive-by shooting on 2 January outside a party at the Uniseven Hair Salon on Church Hill Parade in Aston. The murders had been brewing for at least a month.

On 6 December 2002, 24-year-old Yohanne Martin had been shot and killed as he sat in his Mercedes SLK in West Bromwich High Street. With the street name '13', Martin was a key member of the Burger Bar Boys and was also known as 'Carlito' after the movie gangster played by Al Pacino. Yohanne's brother Nathan – street name '23' – was devastated by the loss of his brother and planned to take his revenge. It was an open secret on the streets of Aston that a gang allied to the Johnson Crew had been responsible, but Nathan knew that the law was powerless in such situations. Two years earlier, a man had been charged with the murder of Corey Wayne Allen, a leading Burger Bar Boy, but key witnesses retracted their statements at the last minute for fear of reprisals. One was jailed for five days after appearing in the witness box but refusing to testify. The charges were dropped and the suspect walked free. This was not the only case of a witness refusing to testify and the charges being withdrawn.

However, the police had had their successes. In 1997, they arrested several high-ranking members of the Johnson Crew after DJ Jason Wharton, a Burger Bar Boy, was blasted in the face with a shotgun and killed in his car outside an unlicensed blues party in Handsworth. On that occasion the police took no chances. Witnesses were allowed to appear in court wearing disguises and give their evidence from behind a bulletproof screen. The trial itself was held 30 miles away in Leicester Crown Court, 30 miles from Birmingham, and led to eight gangsters being jailed for terms ranging from five years to life.

With the conclusion of the Wharton case, the police thought they had broken the back of Birmingham's street gangs, but the case only served to raise the profile of both firms. The Johnson Crew began making up its numbers by recruiting women members, followed later by the Burger Bar Boys. By the end of the 1990s, the turf war between the Johnson Crew and the Burger Bar Boys had cost dozens of lives. West Midlands Police, the fourth largest force in the country, had the second-highest number of armed call-outs in the UK. Staff at Birmingham's City Hospital became so adept at treating gunshot wounds that, when several doctors were seconded for front-line medical duty during the Iraq war, they found they already had all the battlefield skills they needed.

Nathan Martin's plans to avenge the murder of Yohanne were sanctioned and even encouraged by the leaders of the Burger Bar Boys. One of the revenge squad was Marcus Ellis, known as 'E-Man' and number two in the gang's hierarchy. He was also half-brother of Charlene Ellis, who had been murdered in the New Year shooting. However, his brother Nat was a member of the Johnson Crew. Their father, Arthur 'Super D' Ellis, was a key player in the history of gang violence in Birmingham. A forklift truck driver, he had fathered Marcus and Nat by the time he was 19. His relationship with their mother then broke up. After that he became involved with a pretty girl named Beverley Thomas who gave him three children – twins Charlene and

Sophie, and a son named Michael – before that relationship also broke up. At the same time, he began hanging out in fast-food restaurants in the Lozells district of Birmingham.

In the aftermath of the Birmingham race riots of the early 1980s, the West Midlands Police were regularly accused of being over-zealous and criticised for their heavy-handed behaviour, particularly when it came to the random stop-and-search of black youths. There was also an ever-present threat from the far right. Ellis and the other clients of the fast-food restaurant formed themselves into the loose-knit group that planned to carry out vigilante patrols to protect the community and fight the injustices. This became the Johnson Crew, JC or Johnnies, taking their name from the café.

The threat from the far right receded. However, unemployment in inner-city Birmingham began to rise. Soon it was running at over 20 per cent and the Johnson Crew moved from community protection into crime, simply to make a living. By then, the gang was close-knit. Members had often lived on the same street for years and been to – and expelled from – the same schools. Younger members had been schooled in petty street crime before progressing to become fully-fledged gangsters as the crew took a growing interest in the city's burgeoning drugs market. By the late 1980s, the Johnson Crew controlled most of the city's drug supply and were prominent in nightclub security. They were making tens of thousands of pounds a week.

Disagreements over how to spend this money led some members to leave and set up a rival firm based in another inner-city café. They became known as the Burger Bar

Boys after the burger joint they hung out in on Soho Road, and were bitter rivals to the Johnson Crew from day one. By then, crack cocaine was becoming the drug of choice in the city's poorest neighbourhoods. The gangs' profits soared. As the rivalry between the two gangs intensified, so did the violence.

In 1994, Arthur 'Super D' Ellis was jailed for six years for the manslaughter of Kevin Powell, the leader of the Burger Bar Boys. While he was inside, two of his sons became involved in the gangs. Marcus joined the Burger Bar Boys, quickly rising to a senior position, while Nathaniel, now a convicted armed robber, joined the Johnson Crew. Michael joined neither, though would soon become friends with several members of the Johnson Crew. Meanwhile, in jail, their father reformed and became a born-again Christian. But this had little impact on his sons.

Marcus Ellis and Yohanne Martin were close. Together they had been charged with murder of 22-year-old Christopher Clarke, who had been set upon by a gang of 20 men in Fozzies nightclub in March 2000 and stabbed, kicked, punched and clubbed to death with champagne bottles. But murder charges, along with counts of wounding with intent, were dropped in April 2001 when no witness was prepared to testify to having seen the knife being used. However, Ellis served three years in a young offenders' institution for violent disorder. Martin was also sent to prison after admitting possessing a pistol and ammunition. Meanwhile, Nathan had amassed six convictions of his own, including attempted robbery and escaping from custody.

According to a gangland source, 'Chrissy' Clarke was

not a gang member but had friends and cousins who were in the Johnson Crew.

'The night he died,' the source said, 'he was being picked on by Ellis and his crew, who were hassling a girl he knew. They just wanted an excuse to provoke him.'

The Johnnies wanted revenge. Ellis was still in custody, but Yohanne Martin was out on the streets again. He was shot in the leg in what police believe was a revenge attack by Clarke's associates.

Then in April 2002, leading Burger Bar member, 31-year-old Nosakhere 'Nosser' Stephenson, a fitness instructor from Hockley, was shot at as he sat in his car in Lozells, which is Johnson Crew territory. He survived and later told the police he thought he had been targeted because of his association with the Burger Bar gang. He also said he recognised the gunman – he was a member of the Johnson Crew. While ostensibly co-operating with the police, Stephenson plotted his revenge. A few days later 22-year-old Ashai Walker was shot and killed in a daylight drive-by attack in Edgbaston. Walker was a member of a gang called the Raiders, which was closely associated with the Johnson Crew. He had only recently been released from jail and was being driven through Birmingham in a battered J-registered BMW. More than 30 shots were pumped into the car by two semi-automatic handguns. Walker was hit five times in the head, arm and chest. One 9mm bullet passed through his brain, leaving an inch-deep groove in his skull. His cousin and a friend who were also in the car were injured.

One of them described how he was talking on his mobile phone when they turned into Melton Drive and noticed a gang of masked men in a silver car.

'I saw men wearing bandanas and I hung up the phone and stopped the car,' he told the jury. 'I put the car into reverse and shots rang out. I didn't even look and carried on reversing into another car and then some pillars.'

The battered black BMW slammed into a builder's crane, almost knocking the driver out of his cab, and came to rest.

'The wheels were off the ground and then the doors jammed,' the driver said. 'The car finally stalled and as I tried to start it the silver car came towards me. It came and parked in front of me at an angle and then they started shooting through the windows.'

The fusillade continued for a few seconds before the gunmen fled.

Walker was pulled out of the front passenger seat wreckage by his cousin, who had managed to scramble out of a back window. A trained nurse, who lived nearby and had come out after hearing gunshots, spent 15 minutes giving Walker cardiac massage in a fruitless attempt to save his life.

However, in court, the friend who had been sitting in the back of the BMW refused to name anyone he thought might have been responsible for Walker's murder, retracting his earlier police statement. In February 2006, Stephenson was jailed for life for his part in the murder and told that he would have to serve a minimum of 24 years. However, in 2008, the Court of Appeal found the conviction to be 'unsafe' and ordered a retrial.

Six months after Walker's death, the West Bromwich-based Raiders gang found they had a chance to avenge his brutal slaying. Yohanne Martin had recently been released from jail and, according to friends, was trying to turn his back on a gangland lifestyle. He and his brother Nathan had set up a promotional business called Dynamite Entertainment, which booked music and comedy acts in the Birmingham area. To assist in their business, they hired a silver Mercedes. On 6 December, Yohanne drove over to West Bromwich where he handed out flyers for a concert they had organised.

Eighteen-year-old Chantella Falconer and teenager Jordana Plaza, who were both associated with the Raiders gang, recognised him. Plaza stayed with Martin, while Falconer called gang members on her mobile phone. Minutes later two men pulled up alongside Martin's car in a silver BMW and fired a volley of shots. Two bullets hit Yohanne in the head, killing him instantly. The BMW, which had been reported stolen, was later found abandoned in Hambletts Road and two men, described by police as being black or Asian, were seen running away. The year 2002 had taken 27 young lives.

In 2006, Chantella Falconer, a 22-year-old man and a 17-year-old youth who cannot be named for legal reasons were convicted of Yohanne's murder. But Falconer and Plaza's involvement had already taken its toll. A gangland source said: 'The involvement of two girls in Martin's murder changed everything. It meant girls were now fair game for attack.'

As head of the 'revenge committee', Nathan Martin knew that the New Year's Day party at Uniseven would be attended by several members of the Johnson Crew. It seemed to provide the perfect opportunity and a plan was hatched over Christmas. With Ellis in charge of weapons,

Martin recruited Michael Gregory to co-ordinate the operation. His sister Leona had been Yohanne's girlfriend and had a child by him. Known as 'Chunk' because of his size, Gregory bought a pay-as-you-go mobile phone and used it to negotiate the purchase of a high-performance P-registration red Ford Mondeo from car dealer Anthony Hill in Northampton.

On the afternoon of 31 December, two friends of Martin yet to be identified – one Asian, one West Indian – went to Northampton to collect it. Interviewed by the police months later, Hill remembered the meeting because, although the men told him they had come down from Birmingham, they did not seem to have a car. In fact, the vehicle that had brought them had been parked well out of sight. Then they declined the offer of a test drive, which was also unusual, and straightaway handed over the agreed price of £1,850.

Hill also remembered that their phones kept ringing.

'You're a busy chap,' he said to one of them. 'What do you do for a living?'

There was no reply. The buyers were plainly in a hurry and had no time for small talk. However, it was only after they had handed over the cash that they realised they did not have enough money left to buy petrol. Following a little negotiation, Hill handed back £10. The men climbed into the Mondeo, filled up with petrol and headed back to Birmingham. On the way, the Mondeo was picked up by CCTV cameras on the M1. It was followed closely by a silver Vauxhall Vectra whose numberplates identified the car's owner as Nathan Martin. In Birmingham a window-tinter was waiting to darken the Mondeo's windows to prevent any witnesses getting a good view of the occupants. Now they awaited their opportunity.

On New Year's Day, Charlene Ellis, her twin sister Sophie, their cousin Cheryl Shaw and friend Letisha Shakespeare were in party mood. The four girls were practically inseparable. They went to college and church together, and they shared a love of R&B and fashion.

A few weeks before, Charlene, Sophie and Cheryl had performed at a talent show, under the name the Bombshell Ladies, singing their own brand of gritty urban rap. Although none of the girls was involved in gangland violence or had a criminal record, their lyrics were steeped in the harsh reality of the inner-city life they saw around them.

'If you want to fight me look at the door,' ran the lyrics to one track. 'Left your daughter lying on the floor with a broken jaw, you can't get with mini mini me, bash you out the window, kick you in the crutches then butt you in the face.'

And they had ambitions. The year before, they had performed on the Midlands pirate radio station Serious FM and hoped soon to put out a CD. Although Letisha was not part of the group, she was a big fan and attended all their gigs.

That night, the girls went to Rosie O'Brien's nightclub in Solihull. It was full of members of the Johnson Crew. During the evening, one alleged supporter of the gang, Jermaine Carty, also known as MC Wooly, took to the stage. He started rapping, 'bigging up' the Johnson Crew and taunting the Burger Bar Boys. In the early hours of the morning the party moved on to the Uniseven Salon in Aston.

According to Cheryl Shaw, there was something odd

about the party from the moment she and the other girls arrived. It had begun as a small, private event organised by the salon owner, but details had been broadcast on a pirate radio station. A large group of men who had not been invited had turned up and congregated in the back room. As the night wore on they became increasingly rowdy.

'The atmosphere was not like I thought it would be,' said Cheryl. 'There were a lot of old men there. It was quite strange.'

As the numbers at the party rose from 50 to more than a hundred, it became unbearably hot and the girls moved outside for a breath of fresh air.

A fourth member of the Burger Bar Boys' hit team, Rodrigo 'Sonny' Simms, was also at the party. He had been sent as a spotter. Although the Uniseven Salon was deep inside Johnson Crew territory, he felt safe because the salon was owned by his cousin, Selina. In the early hours of 2 January, Simms got on his mobile phone and reported that a number of Johnnies had turned up. One of them was Jermaine Carty.

Around 4am, Marcus Ellis was seen sitting in the front passenger seat of the Mondeo. He was polishing a Mac-10 machine gun, the pride of the Burger Bar Boy arsenal. He handed the weapon over his shoulder to Nathan Martin, who wanted to avenge the death of his brother personally. Ellis then loaded a 9mm pistol for his own use. In the driver's seat, Michael Gregory eased the car into gear and moved off. It was payback time.

The four girls had gone back inside the salon, but again it had been too hot for them, so they moved back outside where about 25 people were taking the air. They had been out there only a few minutes when Cheryl noticed a red Ford Mondeo driving slowly towards them.

'I saw a gun outside the passenger-side window and someone with a balaclava on,' she said. 'The gun was black and square-shaped at the front.'

While Ellis was intent only on shooting men from Johnson Crew, Martin was crazy with rage over the death of his brother. He didn't care who he killed. He saw the small group of party-goers outside. Most of them were women, but that made no difference. There were plenty of female members from the Johnson Crew. Women from the Raiders had been linked as responsible for his brother's death. In his eyes, everybody at the party was a legitimate target and he pulled the trigger. Within a split second, 23 empty cartridge cases had cascaded from the side of the weapon.

Charlene Ellis was the first to die. Bullets smashed into her left arm and shoulder. A third hit her face. It fractured her skull and lodged in her brain, causing a massive and lethal haemorrhage. Letisha Shakespeare was shot four times. All four bullets travelled straight through her body. She was shot in the right arm, left arm and pelvis, while the fatal bullet ripped through her heart and lungs and came out of her back.

Charlene's twin sister Sophie Ellis had been shot in the neck, arm and hand. She was rushed to hospital and remained there under armed guard. Cousin Cheryl Shaw was hit in the hand but released after treatment.

'It happened so quickly,' she told the police. 'I saw the gun then I heard gunshots. I just stared at the gun in shock. I raised my hands to my face. I fell to the ground. I had a pain in my hand. I got up and started running to my right.'

Another party-goer, Leon Harris, was also injured.

In all, 37 cartridge cases were found at the scene of the shooting. They came from three weapons – the Mac-10 machine gun, a Spanish Llama pistol and another weapon, which has yet to be identified. The murder weapons were thought to have been melted down in a local foundry. Later the Mondeo was found abandoned and burnt out.

A few minutes after the shooting had stopped, Jermaine Carty called Sophie and Charlene's brother Michael Ellis, waking him.

'Your sisters are on the ground,' he said. 'It was the Burgers.'

Michael raced to the scene. Then he followed his surviving sister to hospital, where she was rushed into surgery for a life-saving operation. While the doctors were operating, Michael called the only member of the Burger Bar Boys he knew – his half-brother, Marcus.

'Your lot shot my sister,' said Michael.

'What do you mean?' replied Marcus.

'Your friends shot my sister.'

'Is she dead?'

'I don't know.'

Marcus had a hundred other questions, but the line was already dead. Michael called again in the morning to tell Marcus that Charlene was dead. Marcus said nothing. He simply hung up. Then he went on the run, remaining out of touch with friends and family for weeks. Although Ellis had killed his own sister, other gangsters were sympathetic. His primary loyalty was to his gang.

'It's a way of life now,' said another Burger Bar Boy identified only as 'TC'. 'Your gang is your family and people are willing to die for their families. It's not something you can just walk away from – you become a liability. If you're not in, then you're an outsider. Everyone I know has been to the funeral of someone they knew. I understand death in a way that even my parents don't.'

A week or so after the murder, the *Sunday Mirror* managed to secure an interview with masked men who claimed to be members of the Burger Bar Boys through an underworld intermediary.

'We had arranged to meet the gangsters in a seedy Ladywood pub,' said investigative reporter Simon Crisp. 'Paranoid that the police might be watching, waiting to pounce, they insisted on searching the photographer and me for surveillance equipment. We spent more than an hour listening to their shocking tales of gangland life, slowly winning over their confidence until they agreed to show us their hideout, complete with arms.'

Crisp and his photographer were blindfolded and bundled into the back of a white Transit van. They were taken on a 15-minute drive. Bounced around in the bare interior, all they could hear was a soundtrack provided by Ms Dynamite and gang members shouting into their mobile phones.

'The van took a sharp left and quickly came to a standstill,' said Crisp. 'I heard the doors open.'

Still blindfolded, Crisp and the photographer were taken into a boarded-up council house that was packed with state-of-the-art electrical goods and stainless steel kitchenware.

'I was told we were in the centre of Burger Bar territory,' said Crisp.

When his blindfold was removed, he saw three men who

were still wearing their balaclavas. However, one accidentally gave away a clue to his identity. When he opened his mouth a row of platinum-capped teeth studded with diamonds showed through his mask. He called it his '£10,000 smile'.

The gangsters introduced themselves as 18-year-old Renegade, 19-year-old Ghost Face and 21-year-old Phantom, who Crisp said was a bright and articulate ex-grammar school boy. The gangsters told the journalists that the gang had toasted the murder of the two girls with champagne. They also said that Marcus Ellis was not involved in the shooting but that he knew in advance that the hit was going to take place. He also knew who pulled the trigger – a gang member known only as 'Snae'. What's more, they said, Ellis's brother Nat, a member of the Johnson Crew, also knew. They did not know that the victims would be the girls, including their half-sister Charlene. Ellis had since gone into hiding, saying that he would 'rather die' than help the police. His loyalty to the gang outweighed the blood ties to his family.

During the interview, the three gangsters loaded their guns on the table in front of them, training their weapons on the journalists as they spoke. Among the gangsters' arsenal was a sawn-off double-barrelled shotgun, which was kept pointed at the interviewer's legs throughout. They also brandished a James Bond-style Walther PPK, a Smith & Wesson pistol, a stun gun and two 30-inch knives. The meeting ended after ten minutes with the gangsters, faces still masked, posing for pictures with their weapons.

The following day, another meeting was arranged. This

time, the menacing six-foot Phantom and 13-stone Renegade, now sporting a 'Coolio' haircut, brought a woman gangster named Lady Ice with them. A petite 26-year-old, she had her hair scraped back off her face and long purple fingernails. She said that the gang had toasted the killings with champagne and 'bling'. They seemed unconcerned that the two dead girls were innocent bystanders who, the police said, had no connection to the Johnson Crew.

'Those little niggers were involved with the Johnsons and deserved everything they got; it just happened to be that they were the first girls to get shot up,' said Phantom. 'Our firm got those two girls because they were involved. No one can do anything about us, the police are scared to come here and if they did, we would show them what we have got.'

Asked if he felt sorry for the families of Charlene and Letisha, Renegade said, 'I don't give a shit about them – they got what they deserved.'

Apparently, the 'bitches' deserved what they got because of the killing of Yohanne Martin. Although Chantella Falconer and Jordana Plaza had yet to be brought to justice, by then a 17-year-old girl, who could not be named, had been charged with his murder, and a 19-year-old girl had been charged with helping her escape arrest.

Lady Ice said the dead girls had got into an argument with some men at the salon party.

'Nat Ellis didn't think this was right and came from a party over in Solihull to sort it out,' she said. 'After he got there, a couple of serious Burger Boys turned up and were spotted by the Johnnies inside. That's when it fired off and the girls were sprayed by the Big Daddy, a M11. Marcus wasn't there at the time but he knew all about it.'

It is hard to make out whether she was being disingenuous or simply did not know what was going on. Nevertheless, the Burger Boys were then gearing themselves up for a full-scale war.

'We have been told this killing will prompt a war on the streets, but we are prepared for that,' said Phantom. 'There are hundreds of weapons on their way to Birmingham as we speak. In a couple of days, all of the Burger Bar Boys will have weapons like you have never seen, then after these girls have been buried, it will kick off. One of the generals with our firm said a number of us would get killed. We know it's going to happen, but there's no way out now. These are our brothers and we'll die for them.'

Chain-smoking throughout the interview, the gang claimed that they were making £2,000 a week by selling crack cocaine and laughed at news that the government had announced a gun amnesty which resulted in more than 40,000 guns being handed in across the country.

'If we were going out doing a job we could pick up the hard stuff from friendly houses around the city,' said Phantom. 'Once okayed by the boss we could have machine guns, pistols and handguns in a matter of two hours. We are not going to give them up.'

He said that over a hundred weapons were distributed between seventy gang members.

'The Johnsons have more but 80 per cent of their 200 members only have converted pistols and don't stand up next to ours,' he said. 'They may be dangerous but ours are designed to be killing machines.'

He said that there was a special route the gangsters could take around the city, stopping at five or six houses, to get themselves tooled up.

They considered the mandatory five-year jail sentence for carrying a gun a joke.

'The idea of five years inside is daft,' said Renegade. 'Five years is a holiday. When your life can end today, what's five years in prison? We don't give a shit. I can tell you there is going to be blood on the streets. This thing is only going to get worse. There isn't going to be any end to it. We are preparing for war. And there are lots of serious gangs in Birmingham – not just the Johnnies and us. There are also the Baderbars, the Blackrods, the B6's and the Project.'

Renegade maintained that the ordinary police did not do anything about black-on-black shootings – 'they're too scared they'll get blown away too. Loads of people have given them names for the gunmen who killed the girls but no one is going to stand up in court and say who they saw do it. They'll never prove who killed them.'

Despite the short life expectation, there was an upside to being a gang member.

'A Burger Bar's income is a bonus for some,' said Lady Ice. 'They can go to college in the day and earn their money by night. Being a Burger Bar is about rolling with it. You've got to take your opportunities when they come up.'

But she was all too conscious of the downside.

'Up until five years ago I had only been to one funeral,' she said. 'But in the last five years I have been to about 12 funerals. The gangs used to fight with fists, then they went to knives, now they have gone to guns. We are burying our friends.'

It seems to have shocked no one in Birmingham gangland that, on this occasion, the victims were women rather than men. Another member of the Burger Bar Boys told *The Times*: 'The Johnsons showed us [that] little bitches could shoot. We showed them they could be shot, too. There's a new saying in the Burger Bars: "This is a unisex gun". It can kill girls as well as boys.'

As it was, gang support did not prove robust enough to sustain Marcus Ellis, who gave himself up to the police on 13 January 2003. After being questioned, he was released on police bail. He later threatened to sue the police for harassment. Meanwhile, the old loyalties were breaking down. Sixty of the hundred people who attended the party came forward to offer their help to the police.

In April, another mysterious woman, introducing herself at 'The Lady' rather than 'Lady Ice', made her way to Brixton to give an interview to the *Mail on Sunday*. She said that the two girls had been killed because they had not shown the Burger Bar Boys proper 'respect' – gang life is run by the three Rs: respect, revenue and revenge.

'Everyone knows who did it,' she said. 'It was revenge. The girls had been doing a lot of going backwards and forwards for the Johnsons. They had a double life; they have been made out as college girls, but we had our dealings with them. One of their cousins was involved in dealing for the Johnsons. Shooting members of his family is a way of getting revenge. It makes it a lifetime thing between us and them.'

The night that Letisha and Charlene were shot The Lady said she was out mugging when she got a call on her mobile.

'When I heard they had been killed,' she said, 'I

thought: this has gone too far. On the phone I could hear a lot of screaming. I heard people yelling, "Get out, get out." I took the bus down there and I could see all the blood on the pavement and walls. By then the police were there. I just stood in the crowd with the others and tried to blend in.'

She showed no remorse for what had happened.

The Lady said that the Burger Bar Boys were her 'brethren'. She said that she had joined the gang after dropping out of school at 14 and running away from home at 17 to escape a violent stepmother. Gang members believed they were part of a select few and she was initiated in a bizarre ceremony, where the prospective gang member is told to fight their way out of a room full of comrades armed with guns and knives. If they succeed they were welcomed into the ranks with a volley of shots fired into the air.

'The next day PJ' – the Burger Bar Boys' enforcer – 'used a knife to scar my right shoulder to show I was a member,' she said. 'It was quite a deep cut.'

She was then forced into prostitution. At 24, she had already had three abortions and was pregnant again. As well as bringing in money for the gang, sex was used as a weapon.

'We fight each other with guns, with knives and with our hands, but to sleep with someone else's man or woman is a powerful thing in itself,' she said. 'It sends out the message to that person. We have our own customers and territories of control, but to share boyfriends and girlfriends is the ultimate disrespect. People die for that.'

This was even employed in the rivalry with the Johnnies.

'Sometimes our customers buy drugs from the Johnson Crew,' she said. 'That causes a lot of problems. If someone who usually bought drugs from us bought off the Johnson Crew, I was asked to sleep with them. When they paid me it was like we had got the money back from the drugs deal that we had lost.'

But prostitution was the least of The Lady's crimes. She admitted that, during her seven years with the Burger Bar Boys, she had mugged a woman at gunpoint to steal her handbag, helped smuggle drugs from Jamaica and seen innocent people shot during botched robberies. But things had changed since the shooting of Charlene and Letisha.

'Everyone is keeping low,' she said. 'They are not robbing so much. We, the girls, have to get out there more because it attracts less attention. We are all expected to bring in about £200 a day. That's not hard, really. You can do that through robbing, looting or sleeping. I had about 40 men, some you would see more than others. You just got it over and done with. It's not love.'

The gangsters may have been lying low, but the violence did not stop. On 28 June, some six masked men burst into a barbers shop in Aston and fired a shotgun at a customer and slashed him with a cleaver, leaving the man critically injured. Another man's shoulder was broken when he was hit with a blunt instrument. Less than two hours later, a third man was stabbed in what the police believed was a revenge assault.

In an attack thought to be related to the murder of Letisha and Charlene, 21-year-old Tafarwa Beckford, half-brother of the singer Jamelia, who had been questioned over the killing of the two girls, was shot at from two cars as he walked along a road in the Winson Green area of Birmingham in August 2003. He was shot in the head, but his injuries were not life threatening. A week later 34-year-old Denise Marriott was hit by crossfire in Aston. A bullet lodged in her shoulder.

There were a series of drive-by shootings in the West Midlands thought to have been committed by other gangs including the Champagne Crew, the Raiders, the Rally Close Crew and the Badder Bar Boys – ostensibly a younger version of the Burger Bar Boys who prided themselves on being more violent than the original. Nineteen-year-old Daniel Bogle was hit in the head in Smethwick by a gunman who leapt from a passing car. He died in hospital a few days later. Another teenager was shot and wounded in the shoulder in the same area. Then a 17-year-old girl and a 23-year-old woman were shot at a birthday party in Park Village, Wolverhampton.

Meanwhile, the police were making progress in their investigation of the New Year's shootings. The inquiry into the murders at the Uniseven Salon was one of the biggest investigations the West Midlands police force had ever handled. Officers collected 1,300 statements, took in 40 vehicles for forensic analysis and spent tens of thousands of man-hours trying to put together a case.

'What shocked us most,' said one officer, 'is that if you drew a line linking the names of the people murdered and those involved in the case, you would end up with something resembling a family tree.'

Despite all their hard work, the investigating officers soon ran into the familiar wall of silence. Many of the party-goers had seen what had happened but refused to testify. Determined to secure convictions, the Crown Prosecution Service realised people would only come forward if they were promised a level of protection never seen before in an English courtroom. Witnesses would be allowed to testify under pseudonyms and from behind screens with their voices distorted so they could not be recognised. Finally, the police and the CPS found they had a case.

In November 2003, Nathan Martin, Marcus Ellis, Michael Gregory and Rodrigo Simms were charged with the murders of Letisha Shakespeare and Charlene Ellis, and the attempted murders of Sophie Ellis, Cheryl Shaw and Leon Harris. In custody, Martin told the police: 'It pisses me off because the shooting [of the girls] was in the headlines for weeks and weeks, but my brother's death had been in the headlines for a day.'

The trial opened in Leicester Crown Court a year later. Pop star Jamelia's step-brother Tafarwa Beckford was acquitted of murder on the judge's directions as the only evidence against him came from a witness known as 'Mark Brown', who the judge concluded had been lying. However, another of Jamelia's siblings, Kairo Beckford, was convicted of another murder in Birmingham in 2004. The prosecution also claimed that Jermaine Carty fired back at the attackers, but he was cleared of carrying a firearm on the night of the shooting.

Despite doubts about his testimony 'Mark Brown' played a key part in the trial. He was the only witness to come forward and say he saw the killers at the scene of the crime. Brown claimed to have seen Marcus Ellis and Nathan Martin in the Mondeo. Ellis had been cleaning a gun. He said he had also seen Rodrigo Simms in an alleyway talking on a mobile phone moments before the shooting started. But he did not actually see the shooting – he had his back to the car as he made his way back to the party.

Naturally the defence tried to discredit Brown. Under cross-examination, he admitted that he had been convicted of robbery, affray and assaulting a police officer. It later emerged that he had been given 'thousands of pounds' by the police to help protect him after he agreed to testify.

In court, Martin denied being a member of the Burger Bar Boys. He admitted playing a part in buying the Mondeo but said he did not know what the car was intended for. Nor did he have anything to do with the shooting, claiming he was in bed with his girlfriend at the time. Prosecuting, Timothy Raggatt, QC, asked him why he had failed to mention this alibi earlier.

'It's bad what happened to them girls, but I didn't want to get involved,' he said. 'My brother had been murdered, my mum was having a very bad time. I was the only thing my family had left. I lied to protect myself and my family.'

But Raggatt was insistent.

'Your brother was a gangster and you are a gangster,' he said. 'You committed crimes together, you were inseparable.'

'No,' said Martin. 'We were close, he was my only brother but he was trying to reform ... to put it behind him, to make something of his life.'

No evidence was put forward suggesting that Letisha Shakespeare and Charlene Ellis were the intended victims. They were collateral damage in a gang war and were simply standing too close to the real targets. Even though the two girls may have been shot by mistake, the legal principle of 'transferred malice' comes into play. This means those responsible can still be charged with murder – even if they had meant to kill a member of a rival gang instead.

Martin, Ellis and Gregory were convicted of the murders of Letisha Shakespeare and Charlene Ellis. They were give mandatory life sentences and told they must serve at least 35 years before they will be eligible for parole. They were also convicted of the attempted murder of Sophie Ellis, Cheryl Shaw and Leon Harris, and sentenced to 24 years to run concurrently.

Simms was also given a mandatory life sentence for murder and told he must serve a minimum of 27 years for the killings. He was given another 18 years for the attempted murders, to run concurrently. Although just as culpable, Simms was given lighter sentences as he was only 18 at the time of the incident. All four would have the 500 days they had already spent in custody taken into account.

The judge said that they were convicted on painstaking analysis of mobile phone records and they were given harsh sentences because they had shown no remorse.

'The aggravating features are clear,' said Justice Goldring. 'This was gang warfare played out on the streets of Birmingham. Lethal weapons were used. The intention was to kill ... Not a shred of remorse has been exhibited, moreover, and public interest demands the highest possible deterrent.'

Errol Robinson, the solicitor for Ellis and Simms, said they would lodge an appeal. There had been a 'grave miscarriage of justice,' he said, and he branded the trial 'one the most unfair trials of modern times'. All four appealed on the grounds that some of the witnesses at their trial testified anonymously. The key witness referred to in court as 'Mark Brown' had been allowed to testify from behind a curtain. He had his voice electronically distorted and had practically been paid to testify. The appeals were quashed in 2006. In jail, the convicted Burger Bar Boys met up with old-time gangster and friend of Essex Boy Pat Tate, Kenneth Noye. He told them that they were 'mugs' for killing Letisha Shakespeare and Charlene Ellis as there was no money in it. While Noye had served eight years for the 1983 £26-million Brinks Mat gold robbery, he was at this time serving life for the road-rage murder of Stephen Cameron in 1996.

Later, Nathan Martin was caught having sex with a teacher at Whitemoor Prison in Cambridge. A prison warder walked into find her bent over a desk and Martin behind her. She was dismissed. Then a female prison guard, who had been having an affair with a Burger Bar Boy, was sentenced to three-and-a-half-years in jail. Fifty-year-old Yvonne Taylor had first been persuaded to strip off for sexy snaps which she smuggled into the jail. When complemented on her figure, she was persuaded to smuggle in mobile phones and drugs.

In 2005 Johnson Crew kingpins Carl Spencer, Dean Smith, William Carter, Jamal Parchment, Leonard Wilkins and Michael Christie were jailed for the murder of 24-year-old Ishfaq Ahmed outside Premonition nightclub on Bristol Street in Birmingham. Since the murder of Letisha Shakespeare and Charlene Ellis, members of Birmingham's rival crime gangs had been given almost 500 years jail time and the arrest of the Johnson Crew leadership cut gun crime in the city by a quarter.

In October 2005, after Asian youths rioted in Birmingham, the Johnson Crew and the Burger Bar Boys called a truce to unite against the Asian gangs. A black music website called Supatrax featured an anonymous message under the heading: 'One black girl raped by 19 men, one black youth dead, one Asian man dead, one police officer shot, two girls stabbed, cars getting jacked, cars on fire.'

There had been rumours that a 14-year-old Jamaican girl had been gang-raped by 19 Asians after she had been caught shoplifting.

The message went on: 'Word outta street is that members from Johnson Crew and Burger Bar Boys have met to call a truce to recent gang warfare and unite against any attacks from the Pakistani community. For too long black people have had to stand by ... this is a time to unite and stand strong not only for the justice of the young girl but also for the black community as a whole.'

It also blamed the Pakistanis for the amount of heroin there was on the streets, warning: 'Black people and [Pakistanis] have never really seen eye-to-eye and there seems to be a tolerance between the two communities – and this has now gone!'

The rape rumour resulted in the murder of 23-year-old Isaiah Young-Sam when he, his brothers and two friends were attacked by 10 or 11 knife-wielding men in three cars as they walked home from the cinema.

However, it was soon reported that the Johnson Crew and Burger Bar Boys had made it up with the Pakistani gangs after it became clear that there had been no rape. Then the Burger Bar Boys began courting celebrity. In July 2006 they put out a rap DVD that featured former Aston Villa striker Darius Vassell. In it another of the Beckford brothers – Tubs – sits in Vassell's Lamborghini, then makes a gun shape with his fingers, points towards the soccer star's car and mouths: 'Bang, bang.'

'Darius knows some of the Burger Bar Boys because they went to the same school in Aston,' said a gangland source.

Also in the video were members of the Brixton gang, PDC, or Peel Dem Crew, so called because of their favourite method of torturing rivals – peeling off their skin after first scalding it. It was thought that there were family ties between the two gangs. However, they fell out the following year and a concert in Birmingham was cancelled when it was feared that the gangs might use it as an opportunity for a shoot-out.

In an attempt to control the situation, the police set up the West Midlands Mediation and Transformation Service in late 2004 at a cost of £250,000 a year. Its aim was to get gangsters to sit down and talk to each other, rather than reach for a gun. Their model was the peace talks in Northern Ireland, with the Johnson Crew being compared to the Loyalists, with their loose structure, and the Burger Bar Boys being compared to the Republicans, with their strict hierarchy and sense of history.

Though the murder rate dropped drastically, the mediation did not eradicate gang-related crime altogether. In November 2006, drug dealer Omari Rhoden was convicted of possessing £4,360 worth of cocaine and ecstasy in his Edgbaston flat, along with £4,000 in cash, scales, clingfilm and latex gloves, which he said he was holding for gangsters.

By 2007, the B21 Bang Bang Boys had sprung up as a youthful affiliate to the Burger Bar Boys. They wore red clothes as identification and taunted other gangs on the internet via Facebook or YouTube. Sixteen-year-old footballer Odwayne Barnes was a member. This riled rival gang members 18-year-old Damien Belle, 17-year-old Michel Hayles and 20-year-old Nathaniel Darby. They chased Barnes across Birmingham city centre waving knives. Barnes was superfit and outpaced his pursuers. However, they caught up with him in Darby's Volkswagen Polo. Belle admitted stabbing Barnes and was sentenced to life with a minimum of 12 years for murder. Hayles and Darby were jailed for ten years for manslaughter.

The police appealed for calm after 24-year-old armed robber Leon Francis was stabbed to death in his car outside a party at Ruskin Hall social club in Victoria Road, Aston, in the early hours of 27 December 2007. He was a member of the Johnson Crew, known by the street name of 'Trickster' or 'Trix'. Four days earlier 33-year-old Assar Joseph Mohammed Tomlinson had been shot dead outside the Kings of the Road pub in nearby Newtown. At first it appeared that the two murders were linked, but it seems Trix was killed in a dispute over a missing gold chain. Jonathan Hamilton admitted the murder. He used a beer keg to smash the windows of Francis's Vauxhall Corsa before stabbing him. Though Hamilton said he had not intended to kill Trix, he was given a mandatory life sentence.

In March 2008, 27-year-old Nehemiah Bryce was shot

dead in Newtown. Then in May, another concert – featuring Jamaican-born rappers Movado and Bounty Killer – was cancelled due to police fears that there would be a clash between the Bounty Bar Boys and PDC who, in a PR bid following the ejection of Alex from the *Big Brother* house, now go by the name Poverty Driven Children. Meanwhile more gangsters were jailed. Twenty-year-old Earl Savage of Perry Barr was jailed for the attempted murder of Kenneth Anderson and two counts of possessing firearms. He was given an indeterminate sentence with a minimum of 11 years. Savage was said to be a member of the Burger Bar Boys. And Julian Barnes of Ladywood was given seven years after pleading guilty to two counts of possessing a firearm.

The police then turned to more drastic measures to halt gun crime. They introduced a new crack team known as the Serious and Organised Crime Unit to relentlessly target gang leaders as well as other major criminals, from money launderers to street thugs and drug pushers. They were compared to the Untouchables, the force under FBI agent Elliot Ness who targeted Al Capone in 1930s Chicago. They were aware that the original members of the Burger Bar Boys and the Johnson Crew were ageing. But the gangs were reforming as younger criminals took control.

'The Johnson Crew and Burger Bar Boys are still on our radar,' said Detective Chief Inspector Ian Bamber, head of the new squad. 'But there are always people who try to step up and fill a power vacuum.'

In Raleigh Close, in the heart of the Burger Bar Boys Handsworth territory, a 17-year-old was blasted repeatedly with a shotgun in August 2008. A week earlier a man had been shot in the neck in Ladywood in a drive-by shooting. Raleigh Close had seen four shootings in three years and been the site of other attacks in October 2005 and August 2006. By 2008, teenagers in the area were calling themselves the Raleigh Close Crew or the Badder Badder Crew. The police believed that these younger gang members were seeking to take control of the area.

In August 29-year-old Matthew Sutherland was stabbed to death outside the Q Club in Corporation Street in an argument in the street over a gold watch stolen during a drum-and-bass night. It was said that he was a senior member of the Burger Bar Boys. The attack was believed to have been carried out by young gangsters belonging to the new generation of Johnson Crew members known as B6 or Loz.

Hours later a masked gunman opened fire in a revenge attack at a christening in the Irish Centre, Digbeth, injuring a woman in the arm and a man in the stomach. There were more tit-for-tat shootings as the feud between the Burger Bar Boys and the Johnson Crew flared up again. The police had identified 400 youths involved and the newspapers heralded the return of gang warfare.

Armed cops took to the streets and imposed a curfew on the city's nightspots. But that did not save the life of 24-year-old Dimitri Foskin, who was shot in the Newtown district of Birmingham on 23 August. With a bullet in his chest, he scaled a wall to flee his attackers but then collapsed. He died later in hospital. The police appealed for calm saying that they were 'aware of gang rivalries'. It was later revealed that Foskin was a junior member of the Johnson Crew with the street name 'Baby G'. A well-known ladies' man, he was lured out of his home by a group of women linked to the Burger Bar Boys.

A gangland source said the old rivalries were being inflamed by former leaders then locked up in Birmingham's Winson Green and Long Lartin prisons in Worcestershire. Jailed gangsters were encouraging younger members to settle old scores.

'At the moment the Burgers are doing most of the shooting,' a gangland insider said. 'Personal gripes between the leaders who have been locked up are being settled out on the streets by their cousins and younger relatives. Also you have senior members who were sent down five or ten years ago being freed. They are organising the youths who are carrying out the shootings. The guy killed outside Q Club earlier this month was a senior Burger Bar Boy. They want revenge and that has sparked a lot of the violence.'

Meanwhile B6 were taunting the Burger Bar Boys on YouTube. In a series of 'gangsta rap' videos, the violent thugs posed with guns and showed mobile-phone footage of street fights with rival gangs. They were shown smoking cannabis and rapping about their violent attacks on the Burger Bar Boys. This prompted the Burgers to respond by starting their own youth wing, the Bang Bang. They countered on YouTube with images of Handsworth with guns and knives superimposed over the top, and thumping bass music in the background.

On the ground, the gangs' territories became divided strictly by postcode – B6 and B21 – and the A34 Birchfield Road.

Gang rivalries were causing problems for the owners of music venues.

'The problem with urban music in Birmingham is that a promoter can put together a good night and it will be fine for a couple of weeks,' said a spokesman. 'But after a while the Burgers and the Johnsons will descend on it and trouble will start.'

Other groups sprung up, such as the Cash for Slash Money Crew, and Birmingham gangsters began wearing bulletproof vests.

'What is scary now is that children as young as five and six are talking to me, and what they have seen in their brother's bedroom is not porn, it's guns,' said rapper Witness, aka Adrian Burke. 'They are telling me about gangs. It's becoming a culture, with young kids at junior school representing their gangs, ten-year-olds pledging allegiance to gangs who can tell you in intimate detail what's going on in the street, talking about Glocks and semi-automatic hand pistols. These kids suffer from trauma, from seeing people being shot in front of them. And the younger the lieutenants get the more dangerous it's going to get. It's moved from behaviour to culture. I have been nervous before, but it is starting again. And it's scary.'

In an attempt to draw attention to 'gangsterism' in the education system, Birmingham City Council published a document listing 64 primary schools and 19 secondary schools from where they expected the next generation of gangsters to emerge. Locals were outraged at this, saying their children were being 'stigmatised'.

Meanwhile gun culture has invaded every area of life.

'Few shootings are directly to do with drugs,' explained Kirk Dawes, the ex-cop who heads the West Midlands Mediation and Transformation Services. 'Yes, the players are involved in the trade, but the conflict usually comes over issues of respect. Somebody's strayed into another gang's territory or slept with someone else's sister or cousin. At times, it's a bit like Romeo and Juliet.'

A House of Commons enquiry was told that gangs in Birmingham were now more likely to carry guns than knives. On 19 April 2009, 20-year-old student Dominique Grant was shot dead in Birmingham. More shots were fired in All Saints Road, in Winson Green, that evening. The police appealed for witnesses, telling Dominique's friends 'we can protect you'. Two more men were shot and wounded in Handsworth on 4 July. A 23-year-old suffered several gunshot wounds to his body and a 33-year-old had a single wound to his leg. The gunman escaped.

Two weeks later, 20-year-old Julian Gibbs was locked up for six years after being caught with three lethal weapons. When the police raided Gibbs's home in Hockley in July 2008, they found two revolvers under floorboards along with a silencer, ammunition and a quantity of crack cocaine and heroin. He was arrested and later given bail. Then in December, officers on patrol in Abbey Street North, Winson Green, tried to stop Gibbs, suspecting he may have been dealing in drugs. During the chase Gibbs threw another gun away, which was later recovered and found to be loaded with dum-dum bullets, which expand on impact.

Gibbs admitted three charges of possessing a firearm, two charges of having ammunition, possessing a firearm with intent, possessing a silencer and a two further charges of possessing Class A drugs with intent to sell them. Sentencing him, Judge Salomonsen said: 'It is said by others you are a member of the Burger Bar Gang and you deny this.' The court was told that Gibbs was 'likely to end up shooting someone or being shot himself.'

After the gangsta rap videos on YouTube, the Birmingham gangs went mainstream when a nine-minute film called *1 Day* was made in Handsworth for Channel Four in 2009. Complaints were made that members the Burger Bar Boys and the Johnson Crew were used as consultants by the film-makers. An email purporting to be from a girlfriend of one the Burger Bar Boys warned cinemas in Birmingham, Dudley, Walsall and Coventry not to screen it.

'There will be gang members around to watch the 1 DAY movie, on November 6 and there is planning there will be a gang shoot-out and war between the three gangs at cinemas in Birmingham,' it said.

The movie was withdrawn.

CHAPTER 8

THE POLLOKSHIELDS PAKISTANI MAFIA

Glasgow has always been known for its gangs. At the turn of this century it boasts 170 of them. But the hard men of Glasgow sank to a new low in March 2004 with the racially motivated murder of a 15-year-old schoolboy.

On 16 March Kriss Donald was abducted from Kenmure Street by five men associated with a local Pakistani gang led by 27-year-old Imran Shahid. The kidnapping was ostensibly revenge for an attack by a local white gang on Shahid the night before at a nightclub in Glasgow city centre, though Donald had nothing to do with it. Nor was he involved in gangland activity. He was simply chosen as an example of a 'white boy from the McCulloch Street area'.

Donald was dragged into a Mercedes. As he cowered facedown in the rear seat, he was repeatedly punched. Then Imran Shahid leaned over from the front seat and said: 'I'm Baldy. Nobody fucks with me.'

Shahid already had a fearsome reputation and had picked up the nickname 'Baldy' because of his short-cropped, bleached-blond hair. His brother Zeeshan, known as 'Crazy', was also in the car.

Donald was taken on a 200-mile journey to Dundee and back while his kidnappers made phone calls looking for a house to hold him in. When they failed to find a place to take him, they returned to Glasgow. On the Clyde Walkway, near Celtic Football Club's training ground, they held him by the arms and stabbed him 13 times. He sustained internal injuries to three arteries, one of his lungs, his liver and a kidney. He was castrated and had his tongue cut out. Then he was doused in petrol, set on fire and left to die.

The following month, two men were arrested in connection with the crime. One of them, 22-year-old Daanish Zahid, was found guilty of Kriss Donald's murder on 18 November 2004 and was the first person to be convicted of racially motivated murder in Scotland. He was jailed for life with a minimum of 17 years. The other man was 22-year-old Zahid Mohammed. He admitted involvement in the abduction of Donald and lying to police during their investigation. He was not present for the murder though and was jailed for five years. The other three men fled the United Kingdom and sought refuge in Pakistan, which had no extradition treaty with the UK. One of them was the leader of what had become known in the Pollokshields area of Glasgow as the Pakistani Mafia, Imran Shahid – otherwise known as Baldy.

For more than ten years there had been trouble in the Pollokshields area. Once an affluent suburb of Glasgow inhabited by well-heeled industrialists, in the 1960s its leafy streets became home to a tight-knit community of hard-working Asians. However, they worked long hours, and their sons took to the streets and became feral. They formed gangs and territorial wars broke out. Thugs clashed in street battles using baseball bats, knives and chains. Many ordinary Asians were afraid to go out in case they were attacked by one of the ruthless gangs who were tearing the community apart.

There was a running battle between Shahid's 'Shielders', who were Sunni Muslims, and the 'PRs' from Paisley Road West, who were Shiites. But this was not a religious dispute. It had to do with territory and drugs. Well-dressed young men with mobile phones loitered beside expensive cars, while beatings and slashings became part of everyday life. Everyone entering the area felt intimidated. An unwelcome visitor might find themselves set upon by a gang of baseball bat-wielding thugs.

In 1995, Paschael Farren was walking along Albert Drive when Asian thugs shouted abuse at him. Fearing for his life, he took to his heels as at least eight gangsters wielding baseball bats chased after him. He was no match for them. It is not known whether he stumbled or was brought down. It is known that Shahid (who was subsequently convicted of perpetrating this attack) and another youth battered him in a frenzied attack as he lay on the ground. If a passer-by had not intervened, they would almost certainly have killed him.

Farren was rushed to hospital in a coma. He underwent urgent surgery to remove a blood clot, but he was left with permanent brain damage. After the attack, his mind was slow, his speech slurred and he was left paralysed.

'He has mood swings and there is anger and resentment inside him,' said his sister Cecelia. 'He can't work. The thug who did this spits at him ... He is not the brother we knew.'

Later, Cecelia's 12-year-old son was attacked by a gang as he walked home from school. 'One held a knife to his throat,' she said. 'He remembers what happened to my brother and is terrified. We are scared to go out. I have seen old women and girls intimidated.'

After the attack on Farren, the police met with a wall of silence in the Asian community. Meanwhile, Shahid and his 15-year-old accomplice went to Pakistan where they stayed until the heat had died down. However, when they returned after a few weeks, they were arrested. Shahid was charged with attempted murder, but pleaded guilty to serious assault and was sentenced to four-and-a-half years in jail. He also had a conviction for trying to intimidate witnesses – he was said to have put a man's hand in a blender as a punishment.

Even before his conviction, Shahid and the Shielders had been identified as emerging gangsters by a special police investigation. Imran and Zeeshan were the sons of a successful businessman who took pride in being of Pashtun descent. The Pashtun hailed from the North-West Frontier province of Pakistan and were known for their physical strength and their adherence to Pashtunwali, a religious code of honour that predates the arrival of Islam in the area in the ninth century. Neither Imran nor Zeeshan would ever back down from a fight.

The Shahid brothers and Mushtaq come from the same extended family, which arrived in Scotland from the

Pakistani Punjab in the 1960s. Their parents and grandparents were hard working. Their mother, Qudsia Batool Arshad, had arrived from the Pakistani Punjab in the 1960s. She lived with her extended family in Leven Street in Pollokshields. When she married Ishaq Shahid, the boys' father, they took a flat in Gourock Street in the St Andrews Cross area, a tough part of the city. But Ishaq worked hard. He started his own business. The family grew wealthy and eventually moved into a £250,000 house in the village of Law, South Lanarkshire.

After a peaceful childhood, Imran grew into a troubled teenager who was spoiled by his father. At Shawlands Academy, he became aggressive and uncontrollable. He was expelled in February 1992 after beating a fellow pupil with such violence that it required two teachers to pull him off. He transferred to Bellahouston Academy, where his reputation preceded him. There he indulged his passion for dying his hair. Fellow pupils remember it being bright orange. He left in January 1993, aged 17.

After being convicted for the attack on Paschael Farren, Shahid served his sentence in Polmont Young Offenders institution, before moving on to Barlinnie jail, where he spent his time in the prison gym. He developed the physical build and the drug contacts that would go on to confirm him as one of the city's leading gangsters.

'When he came out of prison, he was huge, like a wall, and he was angry,' said a friend who had known him at school.

A friend of the Shahid family noted, 'While the older Muslims daily attend mosque, their kids are more interested in fast cars, rap music and designer clothes.'

Despite his stretch in prison, Imran was not afraid to use muscle. Shahid understood the power of reputation and went to great lengths to foster his notoriety by torturing and maiming victims.

Then in May 1998, a car bomb was left in Percy Street, which was PR territory. A stolen car was left smouldering with two gas canisters and a container of petrol inside. The police believe it was meant to blow up after gas had built up inside it.

A 30-year-old father of five said: 'The car bomb was right outside my house. If it had blown up, it may have killed my whole family. This is a monstrous act ... Sadly, the police know who they are, but can't pin them down.'

The device did not detonate properly, but a fire-fighter called to the scene was injured.

The previous week the PR gang had beaten up members of the Shielders gang. One of the victims had been Shahid's brother Zeeshan, who by that time also had a record. He had 13 previous court appearances, all but one in sheriff summary court. Twice fined for assault in 1997, he was sentenced to four months' jail in March 2002 for another attack. He landed a further 18 months in June that year for breach of the peace and wilful damage, concluding that the 'cops have it in for me'.

That year, former gang member Ibrahim Sharif was lured to Hogganfield Loch in the north of Glasgow and stabbed and battered with a baseball bat. Sharif needed 130 stitches, but no charges were brought against Shahid.

The litany of violence continued. Shahid was jailed again in 2003 after a road-rage incident. After a minor car accident on his way to the gym, he punched 41-year-old social worker Margaret McGregor in face. Then he did a U-turn and drove his car at her as she lay unconscious on the ground. Witnesses saw his passenger grab the steering wheel and turn it to avoid running her over and killing her. He then ploughed through a red light and into another car, injuring four people including two children. Shahid was charged with attempted murder, but this was dropped when Shahid admitted punching Mrs McGregor and driving his car at her, endangering her life. He was jailed for two-and-a-half years. Once again, he was released early, shortly before the murder of Kriss Donald.

Even with Shahid off the streets, Asian crime in Glasgow was getting out of control. In 2004, two Asian youths in a car mowed down two young Asian pedestrians who were standing on a pavement in Albert Drive, Pollokshields. Both casualties needed hospital treatment. An Asian shop was set on fire. A gang of ten Asian youths terrorised an elderly couple, smashing their car windows while they cowered inside. A 43-year-old man was assaulted by two Asian youths near his flat in Pollokshields. He was robbed of his wallet and mobile phone. And an 87-year-old man was assaulted and robbed by an Asian youth who forced his way into his home in nearby Shawlands.

The Shielders also had a long history of war against a white gang based around McCulloch Street in Pollokshields known as the Young Shields Mad Squad. The night before Kriss Donald's abduction and murder, Shahid was out clubbing when he ran into a group of white youths from Pollokshields who attacked him. Shahid himself said that this was revenge for his own attack on Paschael Farren nine years before. Others would see this as poetic justice.

For Shahid, who ruled by fear, it was the ultimate disgrace. His wounded pride made him seek revenge – not on the men who had beaten him, but on someone weak and defenceless, someone who could not hit back.

With Zeeshan behind the wheel, Imran, Mohammed Mushtaq, Daanish Zahid and Zahid Mohammed cruised Pollokshields in a stolen top-of-the-range silver Mercedes. Kriss Donald, a slightly built schoolboy, and Jamie Wallace, an emotionally unstable 19-year-old, were walking down Kenmure Street on their way home to play computer games. Spotting them Shahid said, 'They'll do.'

They were selected not only for their skin colour, but also for their vulnerability and defencelessness.

Yelling 'White bastards', Imran and his cohorts grabbed the two boys. But Jamie managed to wriggle free and escape. But at just 5ft 7in and weighing nine stone, Kriss had no chance. He grabbed the door frame in a vain effort to save himself.

'I'm only 15, what did I do?' Jamie heard him say.

Jamie was told: 'Do you know what pain is – you're next!'

He said later: 'Maybe we were in the wrong place and the wrong time.'

Not one of those who witnessed the abduction and alerted police or Kriss's mum, Angela, could have imagined the horror to come during the next four hours.

Kriss was taken from Pollokshields through the East End of Glasgow to Hamilton and then back up and across Scotland to Falkirk, Stirling, Perth and Dundee. They tied him up and threatened with a screwdriver, hammer and a knife, which they twisted against his body. They also told him that they had a gun. Mobile phone records showed numerous calls were made as the gang's plan evolved. Twenty-seven-year-old Mushtaq rang an acquaintance and asked for access to a house, claiming he 'had somebody' with him. They were looking for somewhere they could torture the boy. The journey was tracked by some 200 telephone calls. Along the way, Zahid 'Zig' Mohammed was dropped off, just four minutes after Kriss was snatched. This cleared him of the murder charge, though he admitted making a racially motivated attack and abduction.

From Dundee, Kriss was driven south again towards Cumbernauld where his killers veered off to the East End and a bleak walkway near Celtic's training ground. A white associate had suggested that the Clyde Walkway was a quiet spot useful for 'sorting someone out'. Throughout the terror ride, Kriss was systematically tormented and stabbed. When found, his body was mutilated by prolonged torture.

The killers' mobiles fell silent just after 7pm and started up again 20 minutes later. Forensic evidence showed that Kriss was held down on the open land beside the Walkway. His arms were stretched out so he was unable to defend himself as the killers plunged knives into his chest, abdomen and back, causing fatal blood loss. Twelve stab wounds were found on his body; another blow had sliced right through his left arm. His tongue and his genitals were severed. As he was bleeding to death, he was doused in petrol and set on fire. He suffered burns to 70 per cent of his body.

'He took it quietly,' Zeeshan later told friends.

Somehow, the dying boy managed to drag himself 50

yards to a puddle beside the Clyde Walkway, where he rolled in mud in a last desperate attempt to save his own life. His path was marked by scraps of charred clothing, soot and flattened grass. His mutilated body lay there until early the following morning when it was found by a cyclist on his way to work, some 16 hours after Kriss Donald had been abducted.

By that time the stolen Mercedes had been torched in a lane in another part of the city; traces of Donald's blood and one of his trainers were found inside. The Shahids' cousin Daanish 'Ferrari' Zahid, who had brought the petrol, got rid of the gang's weapons and the clothes worn by the attackers were found smouldering in an alley.

After the murder, 40 callers to Strathclyde police named Shahid as the perpetrator. They were promised witness protection. As he had fled to Pakistan to avoid justice before, the police contacted the Pakistani consulate in Glasgow and the High Commission in London, who confirmed that some of the suspects had applied for visas. Zeeshan and Mohammed Mushtaq travelled to Pakistan via Paris while Imran went to London, then spent a few weeks in Spain before arriving in Pakistan in July 2004.

Meanwhile, his father insisted that his son had nothing to do with the abduction and murder but was afraid of being sent back to jail while awaiting trial if he surrendered to the police. He had gone into hiding, but they had been in touch by phone.

'When I spoke to him, he was nearly crying,' said Ishaq Shahid. 'I spoke to him on Tuesday after the body was found. He asked me if I had seen the news. He didn't know that he was going to be getting the blame. I haven't spoken to him since Tuesday. He said he was going to be hiding himself. People have told him to keep away. I have no idea when he is going to show his face again.'

Although his son had been violent in the past, Mr Shahid claimed that Imran was a reformed character. After he had been released from jail in December, he had dumped his Scottish girlfriend, Sarah McEwan, who had given him two children. Then he had flown to Lahore to get married. He returned the following month and, according to his father, was preparing for his wife to join him, keen to make a go of the arranged marriage.

Mohammed Mushtaq and Zeeshan Shahid hid out in a small settlement ten miles from Tobateksingh called village 348. Tobateksingh itself is three hours' drive west of Lahore. They thought nobody but nobody would find them there. They were wrong. What they did not know was that their local MP Mohammad Sarwar hailed from Tobateksingh, so it wasn't long before he knew where they were.

The police had a mobile phone trace on them but thought there was slim chance of bringing them to justice. However, Mohammad Sarwar spent a year working quietly behind the scenes to persuade the Pakistani authorities to send the three men back to Scotland as this was an exceptional case. He considered that it was vital to race relations in Glasgow for the murderers of Kriss Donald to be brought to justice. After four visits and meetings with the president, prime minister and interior minister, Pakistan agreed to a one-off extradition.

In late June 2005, the local police raided the village. The two fugitives managed to get on to the roof of the building and made their way over the tops of neighbouring houses before fleeing to the fields nearby. But they were caught and, after a long struggle, apprehended. Zeeshan had been masquerading as the managing director of a clothing firm called Tartan Textiles. But when he was questioned he knew nothing about the business.

Around the same time, the net was closing on Imran Shahid who had rented an apartment on the south side of Lahore. It was in the Shadman district, one of the city's better-off residential areas and he seemed to be planning to stay in Pakistan for some time. He was using it as the base for a credit-card fraud operation in the UK, which was bringing him in thousands of pounds a day. The landlady who rented them a flat said she had never seen anyone spend money the way he did. Again, the mobile phone trace led the police to him. Within weeks of moving in, they had him under surveillance. When he was arrested, Imran Shahid had credit cards in 50 names with him. The two-bit godfather was also carrying a forged UK driving licence under the name Enrique Soprano. He offered the police £200,000 – two million rupees – to let him go. When this didn't work he tried to blame the others for the murder.

Even when they were in custody, the three gangsters still felt they were safe. They opposed extradition, still believing that they could avoid being returned to Scotland. But they were thrown into Rawalpindi's notorious Adiala jail. Faced with a long stay there, they opted to return to Britain. At a hearing in August 2005, they did not contest extradition and in October were put on a flight to the UK.

BBC correspondent Bob Wylie saw them at the holding cells near Islamabad airport, ready for their departure the next morning.

'They were laughing and joking in the transfer cells,' he said. 'They posed for the BBC cameras as though they hadn't a care in the world.'

Back in Scotland, Imran Shahid was also charged with assaulting detectives in Glasgow's London Road police office and attempting to pervert the course of justice by jumping on a blood sample in a bid to destroy it. All three were charged with racially aggravated murder. They pleaded not guilty. The three further denied acting in a racially aggravated manner at Glasgow Sheriff Court when they appeared there on 16 March. Zeeshan Shahid also denied spitting in a woman's face, spitting at a man and head-butting another man. However, court records showed they that shouted racial abuse, swore and spat.

During the six-week trial that started in October 2006, Zahid Mohammed appeared as the crown's key prosecution witness. This led the defence to claim that the case was a 'fit-up'. Mohammed had been convicted on lesser charges after agreeing to give evidence against his co-accused, Daanish Zahid, at the earlier trial. Having served half of his five-year sentence, Mohammed became a crucial witness in the second trial on the first day of his release.

David Burns, QC, the advocate for Imran Shahid, said Mohammed was a 'proven liar ... he has got away with murder'. Donald Findlay, QC, for Mushtaq, said Mohammed had also supplied the Mercedes and probably the murder weapon. Daanish Zahid also gave evidence at the trial, claiming, 'You have got the wrong men.' During the trial Zeeshan Shahid took the stand to deny any involvement in the murder and insisted he had travelled to Pakistan on business. The jury of nine women and six men took about eight-and-a-half hours to find the three men guilty of the racially aggravated murder.

The judge, Lord Uist, described Imran Shahid as 'a thug and bully with a sadistic nature not fit to be free in civilised society.' He concluded that Imran Shahid was the leader of the expedition.

'It was a premeditated cold-blooded execution, it truly was an abomination,' Lord Uist said. 'The savage and barbaric nature of this crime has rightly shocked the public. Racially aggravated violence from whatever quarter will not be tolerated in Scotland.'

As he sentenced the men to life, serving a minimum of between 22 and 25 years, Kriss Donald's mother, Angela, shouted out, 'You bastards!'

In December 2009, the three dropped plans to appeal against their sentences. MP Mohammad Sarwar announced that he would stand down at the 2010 election after he was subjected to death threats over the return of the three murderers.

'They were monsters,' he told the *Daily Record*. 'I knew what could be the consequences for me, for my family, for my grandchildren. But I believed it was the right thing to do. Life is not the same, to be honest with you, since I brought them back. I was subjected to threats. I was told they wanted to punish my family and make a horrible example of my son – they would do to him what they did to Kriss Donald. I received threats to my life, to murder my sons, to murder my grandchildren.'

CHAPTER 9

THE PETTINGILL FAMILY

Members of the Pettingill family in Melbourne, Australia, have been involved in armed robberies, drug trafficking and arms dealing. Their matriarch, Kathleen Pettingill, was also known as 'Granny Evil'. She rose through prostitution and brothel keeping to become one of the most influential figures in the Melbourne underworld. She was a tough old bird, losing one eye in a shooting. Two of her sons, Dennis and Peter, whose surnames were Allen, were notorious dealers in Australia during the 1980s. Another two sons, Trevor Pettingill and Victor Peirce, were charged with the revenge shooting of two young policemen in Walsh Street in 1988. They were acquitted. However, after the death of Victor, his wife Wendy, who had supplied his alibi, admitted she had lied, casting doubt on his innocence.

The Pettingills' criminal careers were thought to have been helped by corrupt cops. Tip-offs thwarted police raids and investigations into their activities stalled. Dennis Allen's ex-girlfriends and other witnesses said that they overheard him taking phone calls from detectives. In her autobiography *The Matriarch*, Kath Pettingill said that Allen was directly involved with corrupt Sydney detective Roger Rogerson who was convicted of criminal conspiracy in 1990. Another detective complained that Allen seemed to be able to do as he liked in the Richmond area of East Melbourne where, as a drug dealer, Dennis Allen was known at 'Mr Death' or 'Mr D'.

In October 1973, Dennis Allen broke into a house in the Sandringham area of Melbourne and raped a woman while he was supposed to have been on his way to kill a man for A$500. Dennis Allen was sentenced to ten years, serving only four. During his time in jail he met drug supplier Alan Williams and went into drug dealing when he was released.

In 1979, Victor Allard, a member of the corrupt Painter and Dockers union and probably a heroin dealer, was shot dead while in the company of Allen. Allard was one of at least 13 people Allen is thought to have killed. These include a Hell's Angel whom he dismembered with a chainsaw, a boy that his mother had taken in, and an associate who had touched his stereo system. While Allen was suspected of killing Allard, he was convicted of harbouring his brother Jamie, who was on the run from the Turana Youth Detention Centre in Parkville. He also faced charges of gun possession and driving while under the influence of alcohol, and ended up in Castlemaine jail. However, he skipped custody while on day release in October 1981 and was recaptured in a Richmond hotel in a room with a prostitute. He was so drunk he vomited blood.

Released from jail in 1982, Allen continued building his drugs empire. On a raid on his house in Richmond in May 1983, police discovered 30 grams of heroin, several bags of amphetamines, a cache of guns and ammunition, and explosives hidden in the back garden. They had been following Helen Wagnegg, a prostitute who had scored 1.5 grams of smack there. After she was released she returned to Allen's headquarters for another fix. Allen gave her a 'hot shot' – a dose deliberately given to an addict to kill them – then sent his nephew Jason Ryan down to the Yarra river to get a bucketful of water. He held Wagnegg's head in the murky river water until she drowned, then dumped her body in the river so it would look like she had died there.

Victor Gouroff, a close associate of Allen, a drug user and former armed robber, was also present during the police raid. He disappeared soon after. His body was never found and the police believe that Allen killed him. Around the same time the body of Greg Pasche, Kathy's much loved adopted son, was found in the bush just outside Geelong in the Brisbane Ranges.

According to Allen's sister-in-law, Pasche had said something 'out of school' and Gouroff stabbed him. When the injured boy turned to Allen for help, Allen picked up a bayonet and stabbed him in the head. Allen later killed Gouroff for not disposing of the body well enough.

Despite the police raid, Allen continued to be the leading distributor of heroin and amphetamines in Melbourne between 1983 and 1987, making an estimated $17,500 to $70,000 a week. By the end of 1984, he had bought ten houses in Richmond and spent thousands on renovations.

His business brought him into contact with Hell's Angel Anton Kenny. They fell out. Kenny's body was found dumped in the Yarra river in a 40-gallon drum; his legs had been cut off with a chainsaw. The tip-off that led the police to the body was said to have come from Allen himself in return for favours he received from police.

By 1984, on the back of his soaring drugs empire, Allen gained a reputation for providing guns to armed robbers. At the same time, he turned police informer under the code-name 'Gus' and many of those who had bought guns from him ended up behind bars. When Jimmy Loughnan was arrested for an armed robbery in North Balwyn, he claimed he had been set up. When Loughnan escaped from custody, Allen wore a bulletproof vest. He was recaptured and later died in a fire set to protest about the harsh conditions in the high-security Jika Jika wing of Pentridge Prison.

One night in mid-1984, Allan Stanhope visited Allen's home and they embarked on a prolonged drinking session. Stanhope touched Allen's stereo. Allen turned up the stereo to mask the sound as he shot Stanhope in the head at close range with a double-barrelled shotgun. He then grabbed Jason Ryan's pistol and shot him again, before slitting his throat just to make sure he was dead. Ryan helped clear up the blood.

In 1980, an associate of Allen's named Roy 'Red Hat' Pollitt escaped from jail in New South Wales and headed for Melbourne, where Allen harboured him for four years.

According to Kath Pettingill, Allen played his part in the downfall of former Detective Sergeant Rogerson through former girlfriend Miss X – her name was withheld and she was put on the witness-protection programme. She said that, on 14 May 1985, Allen sent her to Sydney Airport where she gave a bag containing A$100,000 to Rogerson in exchange for one containing a kilo of heroin. Rogerson denied this, claiming that he could not have been there at the time as he was taking the children of notorious hitman Chris Flannery on a boat trip. Flannery had been killed, allegedly by the cops, five days before. On her evidence, Rogerson was convicted of supplying heroin to Dennis Allen. Although the conviction was overturned on appeal, more charges followed. In 1988 Rogerson was found not guilty of conspiring with Flannery to murder fellow officer Detective Sergeant Michael Drury. However, he was dismissed from the force and, in 1990, convicted of perverting the course of justice.

Dennis Allen corrupted all those who surrounded him. His lawyer Andrew Fraser set up Mr D Investments as a trust fund for Dennis's brother Peter, where they could deposit the massive sums they made from drug dealing. Fraser himself was jailed in 1999 for the importation and distribution of over five kilograms of cocaine.

Aussie-rules footballer Fred Cook blamed his friend Dennis Allen for the drug addiction that ruined his career. One time, Cook took in Allen's nephew Jason Ryan.

The night before his wedding, Cook visited Allen to apologise for not being able to invite him to the ceremony as the media would be there and it would not look good for him to be seen in the company of a known criminal. Even so, Allen gave him four grams of speed as a wedding present. Cook said it ruined his wedding and his honeymoon.

On another occasion, Allen OD'd and his 'enforcer' gave Cook A$1,000 to pay the ambulance crew not to say anything about what had happened. When he came back in from seeing them off, the 'enforcer' asked if he had given them the money. Cook said he had not, but he had given them something much more valuable – his autograph. Sensibly, he returned the money.

In 1987, Allen died of heart failure – thought to be drug induced – while in custody awaiting trial for murder. Soon after, Cook went on Network Nine's *Footy Show* with Geelong footballer John 'Sammy' Newman, who told the story of how he had saved Cook from Allen's wrath on one occasion. Allen had spotted Cook having lunch with a policeman and suspected he was informing on him. A little later, Newman blundered into an upstairs room where Allen and his men were beating Cook with a video camera. The interruption, it was thought, saved Cook's life.

Dennis Allen's younger brother Peter, who was expelled from school at 14, was with his brother in the raid on the house in Sandringham in 1973 and was jailed for raping two sisters. After he was released he went on a drunken shooting spree with Allan Rudd, which ended with Rudd being shot by the police. Allen was jailed for 12 years. He escaped twice, heading Australia's top ten 'Most Wanted' list until his recapture.

Released at the age of 32 in 1985, he began dealing in drugs. Earning up to A$40,000 a week, he bought a flashy sports car and a mansion in the Melbourne suburb of Lower Templestowe. He was arrested again in 1986. Then, after another eight months of freedom, he was sentenced to 13 years for trafficking heroin and conspiracy to commit armed robbery. His possessions were confiscated as the profits of crime. With his brother Victor Peirce, he continued drug dealing in prison. This earned him another six years.

Victor Peirce was Kath Pettingill's sixth child, the son of Billy Peirce, who died after being buried alive while helping to dig a trench three metres deep, when Victor was just ten. When he grew up he went into the family business. He was an accomplished armed robber, a member of the Flemington Crew, along with Graeme Jensen, Jedd Houghton, Peter David McEvoy and specialist car thief and getaway driver Gary Abdallah.

Peirce loved robbing banks. After Victor's death his wife said to the Melbourne newspaper *The Age*: 'He told me he often got an erection when he charged into a bank. He was just so excited. He planned the jobs and then they did the robberies. He got off on it.' She said that nearly every day he would go out searching for possible targets and planning armed robberies.

When two of the mates of the Flemington Crew, Mark Militano and Frankie Valastro, were shot dead by the police, the gang pledged that if any more of their friends were killed, they would respond in kind. On 11 October 1988, Peirce's best friend and one of the gang, Graeme Jensen, was shot dead by police in a botched arrest when, apparently, Jensen was buying a spark plug for his lawn mower.

Early the following morning, a stolen Holden Commodore was abandoned in Walsh Street, South Yarra, with its bonnet and door open and the rear passenger side-window vent smashed. When this was reported, two young officers, 20-year-old Damien Eyre and 22-year-old Steven

Tynan, were sent to investigate. They were ambushed. Tynan was killed instantly by a shotgun blast as he sat in the squad car. Eyre was hit too, but tried to wrestle with the attacker who loosed off two more shots. He was then shot in the head with his own service revolver.

Four men were arrested for the murders: gangsters Anthony Leigh Farrell and Peter David McEvoy, and Victor Peirce and his brother Trevor Pettingill. There were no eyewitnesses to the crime, but the police did have some forensic evidence to go on. One of the shotguns used had previously been employed in a bungled raid believed to have been committed by the Flemington Crew. Peirce and Pettingill denied having anything to do with either crime. Kath Pettingill was particularly vehement that her sons had nothing to do with the killings.

'It wasn't us,' she said. 'I hate coppers but those boys didn't do anything. Our family wouldn't do that. We were not involved. You don't kill two innocent coppers. If you want to get back, you would kill the copper who killed Graeme.'

Nevertheless, Peirce and Pettingill were at the top of a very short list of suspects and the police were determined to prosecute. During their investigation Jedd Houghton and Gary Abdallah were killed in shoot-outs with the police after being implicated by Jason Ryan. Charged alongside his uncles at first, Ryan had turned Crown's evidence in return for immunity from prosecution and went into the witness-protection programme with his mother, Peirce's sister, Vicki Brooks. But Ryan changed his testimony so many times it lost all credibility. Despite having broken the family's code of silence, Kath Pettingill said she forgave him.

Peirce's wife Wendy gave him a cast-iron alibi. She said that she and her husband were together all night in the Tullamarine motel. The police worked on her and, after eight months of questioning, Wendy suddenly told them what they wanted to hear. She said her husband had got up in the middle of the night and had not returned until dawn – giving him plenty of time to get to South Yarra and back. She also said that her husband hated the police and kept guns around the house, and she opted to go on the witness-protection programme. However, when the case came up before the Victoria Supreme Court, Wendy retracted her statements and the men were acquitted. She was sentenced to 18 months for perjury.

In 1992, Peirce was jailed for six years for drug trafficking. On his release he took a job as a crane operator on the docks, but he maintained close contacts in the world of crime. He was the bodyguard of Italian crime boss Frank Benvenuto who was shot dead in 2000. It was also alleged that he took out a contract to kill a man connected with the Melbourne cocaine industry. The victim alleged that Peirce fire-bombed his car.

The police believed that Peirce then moved into the pill and powder market, supplying amphetamines, cocaine and ecstasy. When the drug squad seized a pill press used to make amphetamine-based fake ecstasy, they were told that it was owned by Peirce. But before the police could conclude their enquiries, Victor Peirce was killed. He was shot dead at 9.15pm on 1 May 2002 while sitting in his car outside a supermarket in Bay Street, Port Melbourne. The police thought that Peirce had gone there to collect money from a cocaine deal. It was alleged that he was killed by contract killer Andrew Veniamin, who himself was killed in an argument in a restaurant in the Carlton suburb of Melbourne in 2004. Peirce's funeral in 2002 attracted media attention.

'If I had a gun at this moment, first of all I would get even,' Kath Pettingill told the press.

Peirce's widow and convicted perjurer Wendy received A$153,000 and other benefits in compensation when Victor was shot. Kath Pettingill was critical.

'In the old days you wouldn't have dreamed of going to the government for money. Death was an occupational hazard,' said Kath who, by then, had buried three of her sons.

In 2005, Wendy Peirce gave an interview to *The Age*, pretty much confirming that her husband had been involved in the Walsh Street killings. She said that the ploy to get her husband and Trevor Pettingill off had been thought up by Peter Allen. With convictions of her own, her testimony for the defence would not help their case, but if she pretended to change sides, then pulled the rug out from under the prosecution at the last moment they would have had a chance of getting away with it.

The police denied this and maintained that Wendy Peirce had a genuine change of heart during their interviews but then changed her mind when she realised that, if her husband went to jail, she would have to work for a living rather than live off the proceeds of crime. Inspector John Noonan said that, even though Wendy Peirce was in the witness-protection programme, her husband's family kept in contact with her and eventually convinced her that they could look after her better than the police could.

Victor's brother Lex Peirce only has a criminal record for

minor crimes, while his half-brother Jamie Pettingill was caught for burglary at the age of 11. He went on to become an armed robber, shooting at least two people. He became a heroin addict in prison and died in 1985 of an overdose – or a 'hot shot' Kath believed. His half-brother Dennis Allen was implicated.

The youngest of Kath Pettingill's sons, Trevor, has more than 30 convictions for firearm and drug-related offences. At the age of six, he was put under state supervision to protect him from 'moral danger'. When he was just 12, he and his mother pleaded guilty to possessing heroin. He got seven months.

During the investigation of the Walsh Street murders, Trevor Pettingill was kidnapped by masked men, beaten up and dumped on a deserted road – after being told to tell the police the truth about the slayings. Later he was charged with the murder of Officers Tynan and Eyre. But when Wendy Peirce withdrew her statement, he, too, was acquitted.

Trevor moved out of Melbourne to the family hideout in Venus Bay. Later that year he appeared in Heidelberg Magistrates' Court charged with aggravated burglary, theft and carrying a weapon. The following year, while on bail, he was arrested after a car chase, adding dangerous driving and driving-without-a-licence to the charges. However, these were put on hold to give him a chance to go into rehab in an attempt to beat his heroin addiction.

In 1993, he faced charges for growing marijuana. At the same time Kath Pettingill was charged with drugs and firearm offences. Trevor was sentenced to serve a minimum of 45 months in jail. In 2001, he was fined A$500 for helping a man who was trying to evade paying his fare on the railway, and in 2008, he was fined A$600 for leaving the scene of a car accident.

In her seventies, Kath Pettingill retired, moving full-time to Venus Bay where, in 2002, she was awarded the International Year of the Volenteer Award by locals thankful for her enthusiastic support of the community. She helped run a bingo group whose profits funded street decorations and was an energetic supporter of the local community centre. Locals said she was always willing to put her hand in her pocket to buy folk-art for fundraising.

On the radio station 3AW, Kath said she had changed her ways but that she did not expect to go to heaven when she died.

'I wouldn't know anyone,' she said.

One Venus Bay resident said, 'She's a good old stick ... I wouldn't want to argue with her, though.'

CHAPTER 10

THE MORANS

Some members of the Moran family became involved in a gangland war in Melbourne that led to the deaths of more than 30 criminals, including four members of the family. This became the subject of the controversial 13-part TV mini-series *Underbelly*, which aired across Australia in 2008.

The matriarch of the family, Judy Moran, was born in 1944. Her first husband was Leslie 'Johnny' Cole, who was shot dead in Sydney in 1982. On the day he was killed, Cole had been in Melbourne in his capacity as a union heavy. When he returned to Sydney, he was ambushed and killed outside his luxurious, fortified home in Kyle Bay. He was on his way back from an appointment with a physiotherapist who was treating a wound received in an attempt on his life two months earlier. Sydney detectives believed his killing was related to a Sydney underworld drug feud. He was the first victim of Sydney's gangland wars, which saw eight prominent gangsters disappear in the early 1980s.

By the time Cole was killed Judy had already divorced him and had begun a relationship with Lewis Moran, who became stepfather to Cole's son Mark, who thus became Mark Moran. Lewis Moran and his brother Desmond 'Tuppence' Moran were well-known criminals in the Melbourne suburbs of Ascot Vale and Flemington. They ran a successful meatworks in Ascot Vale before it closed in the 1980s. Desmond Moran was jailed in 1985 and later admitted to a criminal past, largely devoted to drug dealing.

In 1967, Judy gave birth to Jason Moran. His father and uncle thought that Jason had a psychopathic streak – he carried a handgun before he was old enough to drive. Nevertheless, Lewis taught his son how to handle himself. They would spar together and loved belting each other around.

Jason and his stepbrother Mark Moran both attended Penleigh and Essendon Grammar School. Mark became a pastry chef and personal trainer, while Jason was employed at a city abattoir for three years before leaving to become an apprentice plumber. After six months, he moved on to work as a sales representative for two years and remained on the payroll of a jewellery wholesaler for the next seven, despite the fact that he did very little work for the company.

He married his first girlfriend Trisha Kane. She was the daughter of Les Kane, once considered the most violent man in Australia. He was shot in the bathroom of the family home by three masked men with machine guns in 1978. Armed robber Raymond 'Chuck' Bennett and two accomplices were charged with Kane's murder but acquitted.

Bennett had been the mastermind behind the Great Bookie Robbery, which he had planned in a jail cell in the Isle of Wight after being arrested in England. He had used his pre-release leave to fly to Australia to case the Victoria Club. After his release, he took a team of nine men into the outback to train them in commando techniques he had learned in England from the Wembley Gang. However, Les Kane and his brother Brian had got wind that Bennett was behind the heist and told Sydney's Toecutter gang, who specialised in torturing armed robbers until they handed over the spoils of their crimes. This seems to have been the motive behind the murder of Les Kane.

Bennett was attending a committal hearing at Melbourne Magistrates Court on two counts of armed robbery in November 1979 when he was confronted with an armed man who pumped three bullets into him. Bennett died in the arms of his police escort, while the killer escaped. The payback came in 1982. Brian Kane and his wife were drinking with a friend in the bar of the Quarry Hotel in Brunswick, Melbourne, when two men wearing balaclavas walked in and shot him.

Mark and Jason Moran were hard drinkers and had knocked around with other criminals since their adolescence. They became pretty well known in the Ascot Vale and Flemington areas in the mid-1980s.

'They came from a pretty good school,' said one detective. 'They were part of the Ascot Vale crew and it's produced some of the best crims in Australia over the years.'

They were associates of Mark Militano, Frank Valastro, Jedd Houghton, Graeme Jensen, Gary Abdallah and Victor Peirce, who, by 2002, had all been shot dead.

In 1988, Jason was sentenced to one year in jail, with a minimum of eight months, for reckless driving. A driver cut in front of him without indicating at an intersection, Moran grabbed a wheel brace, smashed the other motorist's windscreen, dragged the driver from the vehicle and beat him severely.

'Jason got back in the car and was laughing,' said Russell Warren Smith, a fellow criminal who had witnessed the attack.

In 1989, Jason and his dad Lewis Moran were in the bar of the Prince of Wales Hotel in Ascot Vale celebrating the victory of Coburg Football Club in the Victorian Football Association's semifinal, when a club official answered Jason's mobile phone by mistake. A fight broke out. Punches, glasses and chairs were thrown. Jason was trapped inside with the official who had answered his phone. The man came staggering out, bleeding profusely. Jason had bitten the man's ear off and spat it back at him.

By this time, Jason would use cocaine to pump himself up before committing acts of appalling violence.

'He was very dangerous when he had a nose full of that and a firearm,' said a detective. 'When he needed to do certain things, he used it for a bit of extra assistance.'

On more than one occasion, he fired shots in crowded nightclubs. He pulled a gun on an off-duty cop in a nightclub in 1994. And in Chasers nightclub in South Yarra, he pulled a gun on journalist Paul Anderson when he thought he was eyeing up a prostitute he was with.

When others vouched for Anderson, the gun was handed to someone else who took it out of the club.

Jason became the right-hand man of Alphonse Gangitano, head of the feared Italian Carlton Crew. They dressed like movie gangsters in suits and wool-blend trench coats and drank together upstairs at the Joker Bar in Lygon Street. In 1995 Gangitano gave two women who witnessed a murder he had committed air tickets to the UK so they would not testify against him.

Gangitano and Moran were at a party at St Kilda East to celebrate the release of Mark Aisbett, who had been charged with armed robbery. Around 4am an argument broke out between Gangitano and another guest. Criminal Greg Workman walked out of the door and was shot eight times. He died in hospital soon after. Gangitano was seen wielding a gun. Two witnesses were put on the witness-protection programme but later retracted their statements.

In December 1995, Gangitano and Moran were in the Sports Bar nightclub in King Street, Melbourne, where Gangitano beat a South African tourist over the head with a pool cue until it broke, stabbed him with the broken piece and hit him with an ashtray. When the man was a bloody pulp, Gangitano yelled: 'Who's gonna be next?'

Meanwhile, Moran and Gangitano's other henchmen beat the other customers. A woman had her jaw broken and ten people ended up in hospital. Gangitano was arrested chasing another victim up the road with a pool cue. The police believe the gang were trying to collect unpaid protection money.

The following morning a phone tap on Jason Moran's home recorded him boasting that he had started the brawl and was currently washing blood out of his clothes. When the police tried to apprehend him he resisted arrest and suffered a fractured skull. After being released from hospital, he was granted bail.

The following month, he got involved in a brawl in Chasers nightclub in an argument over a seat at the bar. Moran's wife Trisha called another woman a 'stupid bitch', and the woman then threw a drink in Trisha's face. Moran hit the woman and, when she was on the floor, continued punching and kicking her. He was charged with recklessly causing serious injury and granted bail on a surety of A$250,000, with an 8pm to 8am home curfew.

It was thought that Gangitano and Moran fell out. Moran was beaten so badly that he ended up in a critical condition in hospital. After a second beating, he was forced to give up drinking.

'He's a fucking lulu,' Jason Moran later said of Alphonse Gangitano. 'If you smash five pool cues and an iron bar over someone's head ... you're a fucking lulu.'

In January 1998, soon after the two men fell out, Gangitano was found dead by his wife in the laundry room of his home in Templestowe. He had been shot four times in the head. It is thought that he was surprised in his kitchen. Wounded, he fled into the laundry room where the assassins finished him off. It was thought he might have been killed in retaliation for the murder of Workman.

Another gangster named Graham Kinniburgh had visited Gangitano that evening, but at about 11pm he went out to buy some cigarettes from a nearby store, returning 30 minutes later, after Gangitano had been killed. Jason Moran had been seen in Templestowe that evening. He was interviewed by police, but his lawyer, disgraced attorney Andrew Fraser, told him to keep his mouth shut. As stated earlier, Fraser was later jailed for trafficking drugs.

Judy Moran said that her son was not involved in Gangitano's murder.

'Jason worshipped Al and Al was like my brother,' she told the *Sunday Herald Sun*. 'None of the underworld pointed the finger [at Jason]. A witness described a tattooed bald man entering Al's house and Jason didn't have a birthmark, let alone a tattoo.'

She said she was later summoned to a meeting in Sydney and told the identity of Gangitano's killer.

'He is a small-framed man with evil eyes,' she said, but would not give his name.

Kinniburgh and Moran were excused from giving testimony at the inquest on the grounds that what they said might incriminate them.

In May 1999, Jason Moran was sentenced to 18 months' imprisonment, with nine months suspended for three years, over the attack at Chasers. Judge Mervyn Kimm called the assault 'a violent and cowardly attack upon a defenceless young woman'.

One of the Morans' early associates was Carl Williams. After being kicked out of school, he got a job stacking shelves in a supermarket but soon began running bets for bookies. His mother said that he was a mummy's boy who wanted to be a policeman. He was put off the idea, she said, by the police harassment of his brother Shane, a heroin addict. Shane died of an overdose in 1997.

At the age of 19, Carl Williams was convicted for handling stolen goods and failing to answer bail. Three years later he was convicted for criminal damage. The following year, he was jailed for six months for drug dealing. When he was released, he ran with the Morans but soon began building up his own gang of ruthless young drug dealers. But he continued to live with his parents until he married Roberta, a convicted drug dealer, when he was 31. She had previously been married to Dean Stephens, a friend of the Morans. It was then that Williams and the Morans fell out.

Although the Morans and Williams continued to do deals, they found themselves in competition over the market for amphetamines. Williams was undercutting the Morans by selling his pills at A$8, compared to the Morans' A$15. Carl also sold them the raw materials to make their own pills, but they did not have enough binding agents, so the pills crumbled before they could be sold. There was also a dispute over the ownership of a pill press and the Morans claimed that Williams owed them A$400,000.

They had a meeting in the tiny Barrington Crescent Park in the outer-western suburb of Gladstone Park – in the open, in daylight – on 13 October 1999. Jason Moran seized the opportunity to put Williams in his place. He pulled a .22 Derringer and shot him in the stomach. Mark Moran urged his brother to finish him off, but Jason said that they needed Williams alive if they were going to get the money he owed them.

'We want that bullet back you fucking dog,' taunted one of the Morans as Williams lay bleeding. Nevertheless Williams kept shtoom when interviewed by the police.

On 25 November 1999, five weeks after the shooting,

the Williams's home was raided. Over 250,000 tablets of amphetamine worth up to A$200 million were seized. Williams's fingerprints were found on buckets and bowls holding the pills and their ingredients. Traces of the ingredients were found on Williams's clothes and his father George was found hiding in another room with a Glock semi-automatic pistol. Both father and son were arrested and charged with drug trafficking. While out on bail, Williams planned his revenge on the Morans. Three days after Williams was released, Jason Moran was jailed for affray, leaving Mark badly exposed. On 16 May 2000, Mark's bodyguard Richard Mladenich was shot dead in front of three criminal associates by a balaclava-clad gunman, who burst into his room at St Kilda's Esquire Motel. Then at 8.30pm on 15 June, Mark Moran was shot dead outside his luxury house in the Melbourne suburb of Aberfeldie, seconds after he had pulled up in his Commodore 4x4. A neighbour heard four loud bangs and looked out of her window to see him slumped across the front seats of his car. Mark Moran had been shot twice in the chest. He was just 35.

War broke out. Lewis and Jason Moran planned to have Williams killed at his daughter's christening, but drug boss Tony Mokbel tipped off the police, who warned Williams. In 2001, Williams and his wife were arrested for drug trafficking, but the case did not come to court until 2004, when Williams was sentenced to seven years. Meanwhile, he recruited a number of hit men to deal with the Morans. These included Andrew Veniamin and a man known as 'the Runner', the boyfriend of Roberta Williams's sister, Michelle Mircieca. Along the way a number of minor players were killed, including hot-dog salesman and drug dealer Michael Marshall, who was shot five times in his head outside his luxury home in South Yarra in front of his girlfriend and five-year-old son on 25 October 2003.

Jason Moran and drug lord Pasquale Barbaro were gunned down when Moran was delivering his kids to a Saturday morning football practice in June 2003. Lewis Moran was not able to attend his son's funeral as he was locked up in the maximum security Port Phillip Correction Centre. Graham Kinniburgh was killed outside his home in December 2003.

In March 2004, Lewis Moran was shot dead in the Brunswick Club in the Melbourne suburb of Brunswick. Moran had been sitting at the bar when masked gunmen entered. He fled, pushing over a poker machine and jumping through a plate-glass window, before the gunmen caught up with him. He was despatched with two shots, one fired inches from the back of his head.

Career criminal Keith Faure, who had previously been convicted of several killings, pleaded guilty to the murder of Lewis Moran. He had been picked up after the murder of gangster and convicted murderer Lewis Caine, who had been seen dining with Carl Williams and his wife Roberta at Melbourne's Windows Restaurant on the night before his murder. Faure invited Caine to meet him at the Plough and Harrow Hotel in Geelong. His body was found in the Brunswick area of Melbourne at 11pm that night. There was single gunshot wound to his head. Faure's associate, former WKA kickboxing champion Evangelos Goussis, was also convicted of the murders of Lewis Moran and Lewis Caine.

In 2006, Williams was convicted for the murder of Michael Marshall. Mokbel had been an old school friend of fellow martial arts devotee Willie Thompson, who was shot dead in July 2003 on the orders of Carl Williams. Williams was sentenced to 27 years and told he would have to serve a minimum of 21 years. The decision of the Supreme Court of Victoria was kept secret to prevent subsequent trials being prejudiced.

The following year, Williams pleaded guilty to the murder of Lewis and Jason Moran, and the murder of Mark Mallia, whose charred remains were found in a burned-out wheelie bin in a storm drain. Mallia had grown up in the west Melbourne suburb of Sunshine along with Andrew Veniamin, Dino Dibra and Paul Kallipolitis. Veniamin killed Dibra and Kallipolitis. Mallia had been involved in the murder of Willie Thompson. He then joined forces with the Bulgarian-born drug dealer Nik 'The Russian' Radev, who was shot by Veniamin, again on the orders of Williams. Veniamin himself was shot dead in La Porcella restaurant in Carlton in March 2004 by Domenic 'Mick' Gatto. Gatto was charged with murder but acquitted on the grounds of self-defence. He claimed that Veniamin had pulled a .38 and threatened to kill him. In the subsequent struggle, Veniamin was shot in the neck and the eye. Veniamin is also thought to have been responsible for the murder of Graham Kinniburgh and Victor Peirce.

Carl Williams also pleaded guilty to conspiracy to murder Mario Condello, a lawyer and member of Alphonse Gangitano's Carlton Crew, who was shot dead in his driveway in February 2006. Williams was sentenced to life imprisonment for the murders of Jason Moran and

Mark Mallia, and 25 years each for the murder of Lewis Moran and conspiracy to murder Mario Condello. He has to serve a minimum of 35 years before he becomes eligible for parole.

But it was not over yet. In June 2009, Lewis Moran's brother, Des 'Tuppence' Moran, was shot dead outside the Ascot Vale café where he took his morning coffee each day.

CHAPTER 11

THE BLOODS AND THE LUCCHESES

During a routine wiretap in December 2007, the New Jersey police overheard the strangest conversation. They recorded Edwin Spears, a five-star general in the Nine-Trey Bloods African-American street gang, talking to Joseph Perna, the son of a *capo* in the Lucchese Mafia family. Plainly the new-style gangster and the old-style mobster were on the best of terms. Spears was recorded saying: 'I want you to feel me like I feel you guys, man ... But really, man, love you guys to death.'

At the time, the police were investigating a gambling operation said to have turned over $2.2 billion in wagers in 15 months and used extortion and violence to collect debts. As a result, 72-year-old Joseph DiNapoli and 72-year-old Matthew Madonna – two of the three-man ruling panel of the Lucchese family – and 25 other members and associates, including New Jersey's top *capo* 61-year-old John Perna, were arrested. Perna and 38-year-old 'Little

Joe' Perna were charged with extortion and aggravated assault, both second-degree offences, in connection with threats and attempts to use violence against individuals who owed money or tried to take business away from the gambling operation.

Joe Perna and 41-year-old Michael Cetta, an associate of the Bonnano crime family, were charged with racketeering, conspiracy to distribute heroin and a host of other charges stemming, in large part, from surprisingly candid wiretapped phone conversations they had with the Bloods leader. Perna and 33-year-old Spears, who was being held in East Jersey State Prison, talked at great length. The authorities alleged that the pair were organising a sophisticated scheme to distribute heroin, cocaine, marijuana and prepaid cellphones inside the jail. Investigators said Perna and his associates supplied cash to Spears's brother, 28-year-old Dwayne, who in turn bought the drugs and phones. Dwayne Spears allegedly passed the contraband on to corrupt prison guard 43-year-old Michael Bruinton, who funnelled it to Edwin Spears to sell inside the prison. Mobile phones are prohibited in prison.

'I think it's naive to think that the prepaid cellphones are being used solely to call family members and loved ones,' said New Jersey Attorney General Anne Milgram. 'What we've seen time and time again is that the prepaid cellphone numbers are being used by gang members to orchestrate crime both inside the jail and outside ... It allows individuals on the inside to commit criminal acts, to continue to run criminal operations on the outside. It could facilitate any type of crime, violent crime; it could be drug distribution.'

Purchasers of the contraband were then supposed to pay by sending money orders or cheques to individuals including 50-year-old Francine Hightower and 24-year-old Kristan Gilliam, who in turn delivered the proceeds to Cetta to 'reinvest' in the smuggling scheme. In return for funding the operation, Perna asked Spears to help him pacify another Blood member who was attempting to extort money from a Mafia friend. Spears told Perna to use his street name to solve the problem.

'My gangster name, I'm saying, in my hood is Movelli,' said Spears. 'Tell him I can get in contact with anybody from Jersey or New York ... He's gonna know that there ain't nothin' he could say to you that you can't find out or have him pushed.'

From the taped conversations it was clear that the established mobster and the young street criminal were close. Although there had been co-operation between the Mafia and black mobsters over drugs before, this was the first recorded case of the Cosa Nostra working with a street gang such as the Bloods. It was so unusual that Marc Agnifilo, former chief of the gang unit in the New Jersey US Attorney's office, did not believe that it had the official sanction of the mob. He thought that Perna and Cetta were freelancing to make a little extra money on the side.

'I don't think the [criminal elements of the] Luccheses in general would want to do business with the Bloods,' he said. 'I can't imagine that they have declined to the point that they need the Bloods to make money.'

Previously the mob had supplied narcotics to street gangs on a wholesale basis, but Agnifilo said he had never before heard of the level of involvement that Perna, according to the government, had in Spears's alleged prison drug distribution scheme.

'It would be very dangerous for the mob to do too much business with street gangs, for a few reasons,' he said. 'Street gangs operate in a much more open and notorious fashion, which leads to a lot more street gang members getting arrested in law enforcement sweeps than members of organized crime ... Street gangs, even more than mobsters, tend to co-operate with law enforcement when they're arrested, so if you have deals with a street gang member you really run the risk that he'll get arrested and flip on you.'

However, Agnifilo had left the Attorney's office the previous year. Journalist Jerry Capeci, who has covered the New York crime families for decades and runs the Mafia Web site ganglandnews.com, said that while he had never before heard of the mob working with gangs like the Bloods, he was not surprised.

'Gangsters are equal-opportunity criminals,' he said. 'They will team up with whomever they can in order to make a buck.'

Capeci said he did not believe the mob's willingness to work with gang members suggested desperation.

'The Luccheses are weakened, but they are still a viable New York City crime
family,' he said. 'They still kill people when they have to.'

The Luccheses are one of the 'Five Families' who have controlled organised crime in New York since the 1930s. The family can trace its roots to Gaetano 'Tommy Gun' Lucchese. Born in Palermo in 1899, he emigrated to the US with his family in 1911. Settling in East Harlem, Lucchese became affiliated with Ciro Terranova's 107th Street Mob. After three years in jail for auto theft, he joined Gaetano Reina's Mafia organisation in the Bronx.

Reina was one of the first casualties in the Castellammarese War between Giuseppe 'Joe the Boss' Masseria and Salvatore Maranzano. Masseria installed his lieutenant Joe Pinzolo as the new head of Reina's family. Pinzolo was then gunned down in an office he shared with Lucchese at 1457 Broadway, and Gaetano 'Tommy' Gagliano became boss of the Reina family with Lucchese as his underboss.

The Castellammarese War ended with the deaths of Masseria and Maranzo at the hands of the so-called 'Young Turks' – Charlie Luciano, Frank Costello, Tommy Lucchese, Vito Genovese, Albert Anastasia, Frank Scalice, Joseph 'Joey A' Adonis, Carlo Gambino, Meyer Lansky and Bugsy Siegel.

The group was lead by Charlie 'Lucky' Luciano with moneyman and Jewish gangster Arnold 'The Brain' Rothstein. They kept the old 'Five Family' structure and retained Gagliano as head of the Reina family. However, he withdrew into the background, while Lucchese was the face of the gang on the streets. When Gagliano died in 1953, Lucchese took over. The criminal elements of the family continued making money by controlling unions, while moving into the garment district and the new Idlewild Airport, now JFK. Lucchese developed close relations with politicians and the judiciary. This kept him out of trouble. He spent 44 years in crime without a single conviction.

He helped Vito Genovese and Carlo Gambino take over their families. By 1962, Lucchese and Gambino controlled the Commission and they forced Giuseppe 'Joe Bananas' Bonanno to relinquish control of his family. Bonanno was the last of the Mafia bosses to have been in control since the end of the Castellammarese War.

When Lucchese died, the Commission installed Carmine 'Gribbs' Tramunti as boss of the Lucchese family. He financed the 'French Connection' heroin smuggling operation. When Tramunti went to prison in 1974, Anthony 'Tony Ducks' Corallo took over. He continued the crime family's interests in trafficking narcotics, illegal gambling and union racketeering, and he had close connections with union boss Jimmy Hoffa who disappeared in 1975 after a meeting with two Mafia bosses.

Corallo built up the New Jersey faction of the family, putting Anthony 'Tumac' Accetturo and Michael 'Mad Dog' Taccetta in charge of loan-sharking and illegal-gambling operations in Newark, New Jersey. Suspicious of surveillance, he conducted business while driving around New York in his chauffeur-driven Jaguar. But in the early 1980s, the FBI managed to plant a bug in the car. In 1985 he appeared beside the bosses of the other four Families in the Mafia Commission Trial. He was sentenced to a hundred years and died in prison in 2000.

After the disappearance of Corallo's chosen successor Anthony 'Buddy' Luongo, Vittorio 'Vic' Amuso took over with his ferocious underboss Anthony 'Gaspipe' Casso. They allied themselves with Vincent 'Chin' Gigante and the Genovese family against John Gotti who had taken over the Gambino family with the unauthorised assassination of Paul Castellano in 1985.

Amuso and Casso demanded 50 per cent of the takings in New Jersey. Accetturo and Taccetta protested and the entire New Jersey faction were ordered to attend a meeting in Brooklyn. Fearful that they were would be murdered, no one turned up. Amuso then gave the order to 'whack Jersey' and the whole New Jersey crew went into hiding. By this time Accetturo and Taccetta had fallen out. Taccetta tried to make his peace with Amuso by asking for a contract to be put out on Accetturo. Amuso gave pictures of Accetturo and his wife to a Lucchese hitman and sent him to Florida to look for the couple. But Accetturo was already in jail for refusing to testify to a state panel. In 1993, he was convicted on racketeering charges and sentenced to 30 years. Michael Taccetta and his brother also went to jail, sentenced to 25 years for racketeering, narcotics, extortion, loan sharking, conspiracy and murder.

Amuso and Casso, meanwhile, had gone on the run. They had been implicated in a $150-million scam in overpriced window replacements. Amuso ordered a hit on Peter 'Fat Pete' Chiodo who had been Casso's partner in the business. He was shot 12 times but survived and turned state's evidence. The family had been left in the hands of Alphonse 'Little Al' D'Arco. Fearing that Amuso and Casso had lost faith in him and were going to have him killed, D'Arco handed himself in to the federal authorities. His testimony helped convict Colombo crime family boss Victor 'Little Vic' Orena, Bonanno crime family consigliere Anthony Spero, Genovese crime family consigliere James Ida, and Genovese boss Vincent 'The Chin' Gigante among others. Consigliere is a mafia 'rank', meaning advisor to the family: a low profile gangster who can be trusted.

Amuso was captured in Pennsylvania and sent down for life in 1991. D'Arco took the stand against him. A fugitive for over four years, Casso was eventually captured in Greenwood, New York. He agreed to co-operate with the investigators, but his testimony was so inconsistent that the authorities broke their leniency deal and he was sent down for life.

Joseph 'Little Joe' DeFede took over running the family, though Amuso continued to pull strings from behind bars. Amuso's Bronx underboss Steven 'Wonderboy' Crea became convinced that DeFede had been skimming the profits and Amuso put out a contract on DeFede's life. Fearful that he would be whacked, he handed himself in to the FBI and, in 1998, he was indicted on nine counts of racketeering. He pleaded guilty, was sentenced to five years and turned government witness.

Crea took over but in September 2000, with seven other members of the Lucchese family, including *capi* Dominic 'Crazy Don' Truscello and Joseph 'Joey Flowers' Tangorra, he was jailed for five years for extortion, mainly concerning the supervision of construction sites. With Crea out of the way, the consigliere of Queens, Louis 'Louie Crossbay' Daidone, seized control. He was arrested in 2004. At his trial, 'Little Al' D'Arco claimed that, when he had been boss of the Lucchese family, he had ordered Daidone to kill a man he thought had become a government witness. As an added flourish, he was to stuff a canary in the corpse's mouth to warn others against squealing. Examining the police photographs of the dead man's body, the jury could see the canary in the corpse's mouth and so convicted him.

In April 2006, there was more bad news for the Lucchese family with the conviction of Louis Eppolito and Stephen Caracappa, two members of the NYPD who carried out eight contract killings for Casso between 1986 and 1990. The victims included Bruno Facciolo, who was found in the trunk of a car in Brooklyn with a bullet in the head and a canary in his mouth. There was James Hydell, who was locked in the trunk of a car before being handed over to Casso to be tortured. His body has never been found. After having been pulled over for a routine traffic check, Gambino crime family captain Edward 'Eddie' Lino was killed on a freeway in his Mercedes-Benz. Fearing for his life, Anthony 'Blue Eyes over the Bridges' DiLapi, the leader of the Teamsters in the garment district, fled to Los Angeles. Eppolito and Caracappa tracked him down and he was killed. They also supplied the information that led to the murder of Bartholomew 'Bobby' Borriello, a Gambino family soldier and friend of John Gotti.

While Amuso remained official boss, the Lucchese family was run by a three-man ruling panel – Joseph 'Joey Dee' DiNapoli, Matthew Madonna and Aniello 'Neil' Migliore. With the arrest of DiNapoli and Madonna, Migliore, who had spent more than 30 years with the family, became official underboss. In 1992, he survived an assassination attempt. He was celebrating the birthday of a friend's granddaughter in a restaurant in Westbury, Long Island, when a gunman in a passing car fired two shotgun blasts through the window, hitting Migliore in the head and chest.

With such vicious infighting, it is not difficult to see why the Lucchese family might welcome an alliance with the Bloods.

Founded in 1972 in Compton, South Los Angeles, the Bloods can be seen as the African-American equivalent of the Lucchese. Their origins lay with the Piru Street Boys, who once wore the blue bandana of the Crips gang and were known, for a short time, as the Piru Street Crips. But during the summer of 1972, they came into conflict with the Compton Crips who had joined forces with the Crips from Inglewood and Avalon Garden, and other Crip factions. The Pirus found themselves outnumbered and decided to sue for peace but not from a position of weakness. They turned to the Lueders Park Hustlers for backup, who agreed to come to a meeting on Piru Street. Earlier that year, the Crips had murdered a member of the LA Brims, so the Pirus asked the Brims to attend the meeting, too. Other gangs including the Denver Lanes and the Bishops also turned up. The result was the creation of a new alliance against the Crips.

They abandoned the Crips' blue bandanas and replaced them with red ones; the new organisation was dubbed the Bloods. The Athens Park Boys, the Pueblos and other groups that found themselves under threat from the Crips also joined the alliance. The gangs remained separate units and often worked independently, but the alliance began to spread across the country.

In 1993, an East Coast faction of the Bloods, known as the United Blood Nation, was formed in Rikers Island's detention centre in New York. The George Mochen

Detention Center there, sometimes called C-73, was used to segregate problem inmates from the rest of the detainees. Until then, the Latin Kings were top dogs in the NYC jail system and their mostly Hispanic members were targeting their violence against African-Americans. Under the leadership of 26-year-old Brooklynite Leonard 'Deadeye' MacKenzie and Omar Portee, aka O.G. 'Original Gangsta' Mack, the United Blood Nation was founded, drawing its inspiration from the Bloods in LA, and offering its members protection. The original gang was known as the Nine Treys because they were founded in 1993. Although initially a prison gang, when members were released the East Coast Bloods began to recruit in neighbourhoods across New York. Each separate gang in the alliance is called a 'set' and the original East Coast sets were the Mad Stone Villains, the Valentine Bloods, the Gangster Killer Bloods, the One Eight Trey Bloods, the Hit Squad Brims, the Blood Stone Villains, the SMM – or $MM, Sex, Money and Murder – and the Nine Trey Gangsters.

By 1996, the Bloods had established themselves as a formidable force with recruits numbering thousands. Although they were more disorganised than other gangs, the Bloods prided themselves on being much more violent. They carried knives and razor blades, and numerous slashings were reported during robberies. Drawing blood during the commission of a crime was part of the initiation into the Bloods. They also took up trafficking drugs, and Blood gangs could be found in the New York City area, Upper New York State, New Jersey, Baltimore, Hagerstown, North Carolina, Pennsylvania and Connecticut.

According to some sources, the West Coast and East

Coast Bloods conducted a series of meetings in 1999 with the intention of forming one United Blood Nation whose writ would run from coast to coast. The result was *Damu*, the Swahili word for Blood. However, the Bloods remained a loosely structured association of small street gangs, known as 'sets' (as referred to previously), who have adopted a common gang culture. Each set has its own leader and generally operates independently from the others. Most members are African-American males, although some sets have recruited females and members from other ethnic backgrounds. They mainly recruit school-age kids in predominantly poor African-American areas. Gang membership offers a youth protection and gives them a sense of belonging. For economically disadvantaged kids it also offers the trappings of gang life – cash, bling and expensive sports clothing. The Bloods wear 'Starter' jackets in red, which has become the Bloods' colour right across the US. Their favourite teams include the San Francisco Forty Niners, the Philadelphia Phillies and the Chicago Bulls. They are also known to wear Dallas Cowboys clothing whose logo contains a five-pointed star, which has become a gang icon.

Members range in age from early teens to mid-twenties, however some hold leadership positions into their late twenties and occasionally thirties. While the Bloods have no national leader, individual sets have a strong hierarchical structure. The leader is typically an older member with a more extensive criminal background who asserts himself by developing and managing the gang's criminal enterprises. He may do this by his personal charisma, more often through his reputation for ruthlessness and violence. Under his command are 'soldiers' who exhibit a strong commitment to their set and gain the respect of other gang members by their willingness to use violence against anyone who 'disrespects' the set. There are also 'associates' who are not full members, but they identify with the gang and take part in criminal activities. The gang's women are usually associate members. They are expected to carry weapons, hold drugs or prostitute themselves to make money for their male counterparts.

In the year 2000, the Bloods became affiliated with People Nation, an alliance of gangs formed in Chicago. People Nation began in 1978, when Bobby Gore of the Vice Lords, Gustavo Colon of the Latin Kings and Jeff Fort of El Rukns, later known as the Black P. Stone, allied their gangs in opposition to the Folk Nation, another Chicago-based alliance of gangs that spread throughout the US and Canada. The Insane Unknowns, Spanish Lords, Latin Counts, Bishops and Cobra Stones, later known as Mickey Cobras, joined. Soon after the South Side Popes and the Gaylords signed up, followed finally by the Bloods. The African-American gangs turned to Islam, while the Latin gangs remained strictly Catholic. People Nation gangs have become particularly strong in prisons across the US, where they offer members protection.

Members of People Nation and its affiliates wear an earring in the left ear. They have the left leg of their trousers rolled up and have their baseball cap tilted to the left. Gangs identify themselves by hand signs. The People Nation hand sign is thrown to the left shoulder. However, when the gang members fold their arms, they do it in a manner that is pointed to the right. Gang graffiti incorporates a five-pointed star that originated with the Black P. Stone Ranger Nation, one of the larger street gangs that began as the Blackstone Rangers in the 1950s. They have seven branches in Chicago – Gangster Stones, Jet Black Stones, Rubinite Stones, Familia Stones, Puerto Rican Stones, Corner Stones and Black P. Stones who also call themselves the El Rukn tribe. These gangs were originally formed to oppose white supremacists groups such as the Ku Klux Klan, the Aryan Brotherhood and white-power skinheads, and allied themselves with black separatist groups.

Along with the five-pointed star, the People Nation also use a five-pointed crown, a die showing its five sides, a 3D pyramid which has five points, a crescent moon with its concave side facing to the right, sometimes with a small five-pointed star to the right of the moon, and a symbol resembling the Playboy bunny. These symbols are seen in graffiti and tattoos, and on jewellery and clothing. Graffiti artists also draw a pitchfork pointed downwards as a symbol of disrespect to the Folk Nation. People Nation's slogan 'high five, six must die' refers to the superiority of the five-pointed star over the six-pointed star of the Folk Nation alliance. Other versions include 'five in the sky, six must die' and 'five poppin, six droppin'. Their greeting is 'All is well'.

Bloods refer to each other as Dawg. United Blood Nation or East Coast Bloods initiates often receive a dog-paw mark – three dots usually burned with a cigarette on their upper arm or right shoulder. Some Bloods carry a tattoo of a dog, usually the type of bulldog seen in the Mack Truck logo, or a bull. They also use the acronym

MOB – Member of Blood or Money Over Bitches – to identify themselves, carrying the letters on their skin as a burn scar or a tattoo. Bloods greet each other with the word 'Blood' and often avoid using words with the letter 'C'. They also use hand signs to communicate with one another. These may be a singular movement, like the letter 'B' in American sign language, or a series of movements using one or both hands for more complex phrases.

In 2003, the New York Police Department led a crackdown on a Bloods gang selling drugs in the Hunts Point section of the Bronx, easily identified by their red clothing. Undercover policemen bought heroin, crack and powdered cocaine from gang members on 62 occasions at four locations in Hunts Point. The police estimated that a total of $1.5 million worth of drugs were sold from those four locations in a year.

'Hunts Point is a particularly difficult area for our undercovers to work in,' said Police Commissioner Raymond W. Kelly. 'The gang members are deeply suspicious and extremely violent.'

The police seized an assault rifle and a handgun, along with 899 glassine envelopes of heroin, two ounces of crack cocaine and 1.5 ounces of powdered cocaine.

Commissioner Kelly estimated that there were 17,000 members of street gangs in New York City, compared with 40,000 in Chicago and 50,000 in Los Angeles. In the Hunters Point operation, the police arrested just 19 of them for drug and firearms offences, though four were already in custody on other charges. A grand jury handed down ten indictments with 42 counts and gang members faced up to 25 years in prison.

The website insideprison.com lists over 118 Bloods gangs, including the ethnically Hmong Suicidal Gangster Bloods in Minneapolis-St Paul, the True Portuguese Bloods in Toronto's Little Portugal and the Circle City Neighborhood Bloods, or CCNHB, in Indianapolis. The two c's have a line through them like a cent sign. They wear red NY Yankee hats, meaning Neighborhood Youngstaz, and Cincinnati Reds hats because of the red 'C'. 'Stop Snitchin' T-shirts identify all Bloods in Indianapolis, which was originally the shirt of the Dip-Set – a set of the Nine Trey in Harlem. In 2003, the CCNHB made an alliance with the 317 Bloods and Rollins 20 to form the Dub Trey Gangsters.

The website also identified individuals with alleged 'executive' connections. These include OG (Original Gangster) Mack, or 'The Big Homie', founder of the Rikers Island Nine Trey. When this man was released, the Universal Blood Nation became the East Coast chapter of the Bloods street gang. However, in 2003, he was sentenced to 50 years in prison for murder conspiracy, credit-card fraud and selling drugs.

Then there is Sherman Adams, aka 'Sherm Da Worm', a native of Queens and a leader of the Rikers Island Blood set in the 1990s. He is now serving two life sentences. In 1997, he was the highest-ranking Blood member inside Rikers' Adolescent Reception and Detention Center. As a teenager, he was dubbed the 'Superior of All Adolescents' because of his penchant for slicing rivals with a razor. As a result, he was assigned the corrections department's highest security rating, Code 2. Even prison officers were wary of him. They put black mitts on his hands whenever he left his cell for court appearances or to see visitors to prevent him wielding a blade. Over the years, he has promoted the idea that the Bloods represent the interests of African-American inmates in jail, raising the Bloods above the lowly status of ordinary street gangs.

In 2008, 450 state and city police attempted to clamp down on the Mob Piru, a Bloods set responsible for a number of drive-by shootings in Compton, Lynwood and other parts of Los Angeles County. Twenty-four of the set's estimated 200 members were arrested and 18 guns seized in Operation Killen Court which aimed to prevent a shoot-out between Mob Piru and the Insane Crips.

The following year, four Bloods from the 662 Boss Piru gang were jailed in Washington, DC, for kidnapping and beating an 18-year-old female gang member, who was pregnant because she 'had been straying from gang activities' the court papers said. The gang had forced her into prostitution. Meanwhile, a Bloods set in North Baltimore firebombed the home of a 60-year-old community association president who complained about their drug dealing. They did this because they decided that shooting her in the head would not intimidate the neighbourhood enough.

CHAPTER 12

THE CRIPS

The Crips are the sworn enemies of the Bloods, first in Los Angeles and then across the western states. They have some 35,000 members in California, Missouri, Oklahoma and Texas, though Crips gangs can be found in every city of the United States. To control the drugs trade on the West Coast, they had broadened their membership to include Caucasians, Hispanics and Asians, as well as the original African-Americans.

The Crips can trace their origins back to a meeting in 1969 between two 15-year-olds – Raymond Lee Washington and Stanley 'Tookie' Williams. They agreed to ally their gangs from the west and east sides of South Central LA, forming what became the Crips, to fight neighbouring street gangs. In his memoir *Blue Rage, Black Redemption*, Williams looked back further to the roots of the gang in the 1950s and 60s. During the 1940s, African-Americans had flocked to Los Angeles from the South. In

1941, President Franklin Roosevelt passed Executive Order 8801, banning racial discrimination in wartime defence industries. Companies such as Goodyear, Firestone, Chrysler and Ford all set up factories in south Los Angeles. Between 1940 and 1970, five million African-Americans left the heavily segregated South for cities in the North and West. During that time, Los Angeles's black population grew from 63,744 to nearly 736,000.

Between 1944 and 1948, the newly named South Central area was booming. It was the only district in the city where African-Americans were allowed to own property, and Central Avenue was home to black-owned businesses and a thriving jazz and R&B music scene. Elsewhere racially restrictive housing covenants, enforced by the law, police authorities and white homeowners, kept LA's schools and communities strictly segregated and denied people of colour the right to own homes.

Housing projects in Watts, initially built for war industry employees, were planned with racial integration in mind. Residents of the larger projects, such as Imperial Courts and Jordan Downs – both built in 1944 – were by and large African-Americans. In 1948, the Supreme Court banned racial restrictive housing covenants. This meant that African-Americans could spread out from the increasingly overcrowded South Central. Meanwhile the construction of the freeway system meant that affluent whites could flee to the outer suburbs and still do business in the city.

By the 1950s, South Central was suffering from the post-World War II economic decline. This led to joblessness and poverty. Racial segregation led to the formation of black 'street clubs' by young African-American men. The Slauson gang, the first known gang in this area, was formed by boys who were not allowed to join the whites-only Boy Scout troop. Bunchy Carter, later the leader of the LA Chapter of the Black Panthers, started out as a member of the Slausons.

In response to violent attacks by white gangs such as the Spook Hunters in Huntington Park and South Gate, young black Angelenos (residents of Los Angeles) formed street clubs such as the Devil Hunters, the Farmers and the Huns. White gangs and black gangs fought in neighbourhoods where the racial complexion was changing. Many of the gangs were organised geographically by housing projects.

Despite the passing of the Civil Rights Act, California passed new legislation to maintain segregation in housing. In 1965, simmering resentment exploded in the Watts Riots. Thirty-four people died, over a thousand were wounded and millions of dollars worth of property was damaged. In the aftermath of the riots, the black street gangs united against police brutality. The Black Power Movement gained strength nationally, and violent gang activity decreased in LA, as former gang members joined the Black Panther Party and other militant organisations. However, a campaign by the FBI and the Los Angeles Police Department resulted in the deaths of two leaders of the Black Panther Party and the incarceration of others.

In the 1970s, factories closed, leaving South Central in steep economic decline. In the absence of the Black Panthers, crime took over. Raymond Washington and Tookie Williams wanted to try and emulate the older gangs, continuing the revolutionary ideals of the Panthers and protecting their communities. Their alliance took its name from Central Avenue and, as the membership was so young, became known as the Baby Avenues. They then became known as the Avenue Cribs. Other names were suggested – the Black Overlords and the Assassins – but they stuck with 'Cribs' again because of the conspicuous youth of the membership. 'Cribs' then morphed into 'Crips' as gang members began carrying around canes to display their 'pimp' status and people in the neighbourhood began calling them cripples, or 'Crips' for short. Williams, in his memoir, further discounted claims that the group was a spin-off of the Black Panther Party or was formed for a community agenda. The name, he said, 'depicted a fighting alliance against street gangs – nothing more, nothing less.' Williams, who attended Washington High School, led the West Side Crips, while Washington, who went to Fremont High School, was the leader of the East Side Crips.

They used to hang out with other youths in what is now Jesse Owens Park, where the locals would go for Friday night dances. These assemblies eventually stopped due to violence. Raymond Washington and Tookie Williams would also get together with other allies at the drive-in Rio Theater to cement their alliance.

Crip members initiate into the gang by committing a crime in front of gang witnesses. This initiation process is called 'loc'ing-in'. Female members could do the same or become 'sexed-in' by having sex with several older members. Early members of Raymond Washington's East Side crew included Curtis 'Buddha' Morrow who first wore the blue bandana, Williams recalled. It co-ordinated with his blue Levi jeans, blue shirt and dark blue braces. A blue bandana was worn in memory of Buddha after he was shot dead in 1973 and blue became the colour of the Crips.

Crips usually wear jogging suits and tennis shoes, professional sports team jackets and caps bearing the names of Los Angeles teams, sometimes with Adidas sweatshirts. Dickey brand cotton work trousers or bib-style overalls are also popular, along with Nike trainers and British Knights shoes.

At the time, Avalon Gardens were fighting the Walnuts. When Jimel Barnes of the Avalon Gardens was shot, they joined the Crips for protection. More gangs joined until they outnumbered non-Crip gangs by three to one. They took on the LA Brims, Athens Park Boys, the Bishops, The Drill Company and the Denver Lanes. Then when the Bloods sprang up in the summer of 1972, fist-fights gave way to guns. By 1974, there were 70 gang-related homicides as the Crips and Bloods spread across South Central Los Angeles, Compton and Inglewood, taking in nearly 30 square miles.

The early line-up of Crip gangs in Los Angeles included the East Side Crips, the West Side Crips, the Compton Crips, the Avalon Garden Crips, the 43rd Street Crips, the Grandee Crips, the Harlem Crips, the Hoover Crips and the Inglewood Crips. The original nine Crips gangs in 1972 grew to about 45 by 1978, according to LA County Probation Department statistics. The LA County Sheriffs Department counted 109 Crips outfits in LA County by 1982, and by the late 1990s streetgangs.com counted 199 individual Crips gangs active in LA County.

Crips founder Raymond Washington was shot and killed

on San Pedro and 64th Street in South Central on 9 August 1979. His murder remains unsolved. He was just 25. That same year, Stanley 'Tookie' Williams was convicted of four murders, committed during robberies, and would remain in prison for the rest of his life.

By the early 1980s the gang was heavily involved with the drugs trade. Some of these Crips sets began to produce and distribute PCP (phencyclidine) – also known as 'angel dust' – within the city. They also began to distribute marijuana and amphetamines throughout Los Angeles. Freeway Ricky Ross himself worked out of a house on 74th Street and Hoover, known as Hoovas. Soon lines of up to 70 people were seen queuing at a crack house on 79th Street. Both the Crips and the Bloods were into crack production. The murder and the incarceration rates soared.

The huge profits resulting from the distribution of crack encouraged Crips' members to seek out new markets in other cities and states. While gang membership began to decline in South Central LA due to a demographic change, Crips gangs sprung up in other parts of California and the United States, with disadvantaged young men taking the Crips name and adopting their lifestyle. Even abroad, youths started copycat Crip gangs, some of which had nothing to do with the original group in Los Angeles.

During the 1980s, several Crip and Blood gangs developed in the Central American country of Belize. Many migrated to the United States during the late 1980s, settling throughout the West Coast and in the East Coast states of New York, New Jersey, Florida, North Carolina, South Carolina and Georgia. In 1989, several large Belizean families arrived in New York's Harlem and youths from these families created the Harlem Mafia Crips. They have since helped establish several other Crip gangs such as the Rolling 30s Crips, 92 Hoover Crips and Rolling 60s Crips. Crips on the East Coast wear blue and clear beads or blue and white beads around their necks, blue jeans and white shirts. Like their West Coast brothers they are enemies of the Bloods. East Coast Crips have also affiliated with the Folk Nation gangs. Started in Chicago, the Folk Nation alliance spread through the prison system much like the People Nation did. Most Folk Nation gangs – excluding the Imperial Gangsters and the Insane Spanish Cobras – use the six-pointed star as a symbol. The Gangster Disciples, Black Disciples, Spanish Gangster Disciples, Satan Disciples and Maniac Latin Disciples also use the pitchfork as a symbol, though this is now depicted in Bloods graffiti with the tines down as a mark of disrespect, as mentioned previously. Other allied gangs include the La Raza Nation, Gangster Two Six, Latin Eagles, Simon City Royals and the Harrison Gents.

Crips refer to each other as 'Cuzz' and use the letter 'c' to replace the letter 'b' in their conversations and writings as B is associated with their enemy the Bloods and must be disrespected. As the Bloods use 'CK' to stand for 'Crip killer', the Crips substitute 'cc' for 'ck', and 'bk' – Blood killer – for 'b', so 'kick back' is rendered 'kicc bkacc'. Graffiti marks their territorial boundaries and they identify themselves with complex hand signals known as 'flashing'.

In 1991, gangster life came to the big screen with the Oscar-nominated movie *Boyz n the Hood*, written and directed by South Central native John Singleton. It told the story of three friends growing up in the neighbourhood, offering a realistic portrait of inner-city life. It starred Ice Cube, another native of South Central. Along with albums like N.W.A.'s *Straight Outta Compton* and films like *Menace II Society*, *Boyz n the Hood* brought the street gangs of South Central to worldwide attention.

The world also got to learn of racism in Los Angeles in March 1991 when four white Los Angeles' police officers were videoed beating black motorist Rodney King. The officers were charged with using excessive force. When they were acquitted by a jury of ten whites, one Latino and one Asian, riots broke out leading to 53 deaths, 2,383 injuries, more than 7,000 fires, damage to 3,100 businesses and a financial loss of nearly $1 billion.

However, the Rodney King case united the black gangs. The day before the Rodney King verdict set the city ablaze, the Crips and Bloods agreed a truce. This was brokered by older gang members who did not want their children to face the same gang violence they had endured. There were celebrations and families and friends were once again able to visit each other in different projects without fear. After the riots, the city promised a six-billion-dollar investment programme called Rebuild LA, which aimed to create 74,000 new jobs in South Central. But these jobs did not materialise and the programme shut down within a year. Much of the optimism generated disappeared in October 1991 when Dewayne Holmes, one of those who brokered the truce, was jailed for seven years for allegedly stealing $10. Dewayne believes he was targeted. However, there was a reduction in gang-related homicides and in 1993 a national gang peace summit was held in Chicago attended by hundreds of gang members from different cities across the country.

In Los Angeles the racial mix was changing. By 1996 there were more than 600 Latino gangs in Los Angeles County and an Asian gang boasted a membership of more than 20,000. During the 1990s, South Central lost nearly a half of its black population and by the year 2000 was 47 per cent Latino. This led to tensions and racially provoked gang violence.

Nationally Crips' membership continued to increase throughout the 1980s, making it one of the largest street-gang associations in the country. By 1999, there were at least 600 Crips sets with more than 30,000 members involved in transporting drugs in the United States. The Crips now have over 800 sets with approximately 35,000 members and associate members. There are more than 13,000 members in Los Angeles alone. The states with the highest estimated number of Crips sets are California, Missouri, Oklahoma and Texas. Members are still usually young African-American men, but there are now white, Hispanic and Asian members.

In 2003 Los Angeles City Council voted to change the area's name from South Central to South Los Angeles in an effort to rid the area of the stigma the name attracted. With harsher sentencing laws and the Federal government's 'war on drugs', imprisonment rates soared. A survey in 2003 found that one in four African-American men would go to prison at some time in their life. California also had the largest number of female prisoners in the US – most of whom were mothers of young children. South LA had the largest number of prison releases. Even though the area contains just ten per cent of the city's population, in 2005 it was home to one out of four of its prison parolees.

Things were even worse in Watts, where generations of project residents have gone without jobs and economic opportunities and 75 per cent of the neighbourhood's adult African-American males will be incarcerated in their lifetimes. Watts residents have a 1 in 250 chance of being murdered, compared to 1 in 18,000 for the average American. Nearly half of the neighbourhood's children suffer from post-traumatic stress disorder.

Not only do the Crips take on the Bloods and other gangs, they fight each other. The Rollin' 60s and 83rd Street Gangster Crips have been acrimonious rivals since 1979. In Watts, the Grape Street Watts Crips from Jordan Downs and the PJ Crips from Imperial Court have such a bitter feud that the PJ Crips even teamed up with the local Bloods set, the Bounty Hunter Bloods from Nickerson Gardens, to take them on. Meanwhile, the Grape Street Crips dropped the Crips colour blue and began wearing purple to further muddy the water.

Before the truce, there were 25 homicides a year in the projects. In 1997, at the height of the treaty, this had dropped to just four. But then the murder rate began to climb again. In the first half of 2005, there were at least seven killings in and around the projects, dozens of shootings and a reported 187 violent crimes. Gone were the days when the homies played football together or enjoyed rowdy parties.

Although the 1,066-unit Nickerson Gardens was the largest housing project west of the Mississippi, it was nothing like the notorious 16-storey Robert Taylor Homes on the South Side of Chicago, which were finally demolished in 2007. Nickerson Gardens was a collection of two-storey buildings with small patches of lawn that even had rose beds in front of them. Visitors said that driving through they appeared pleasant. However, those who lingered noted the poverty and aura of hopelessness. Since 1990, nearly one-third of South LA residents have been living below the poverty line, just miles from some of the country's wealthiest neighbourhoods.

Although the peace treaty never officially ended, the law-enforcement agencies said that it had become increasingly shaky as a new generation of gang members came of 'shooting age' – which in South Central is about 13 to 16. Word spread among the residents of Nickerson Gardens that it was not wise to visit Jordan Downs any more, and people from Jordan Downs were afraid to go to the Nickersons or Imperial Courts.

'We ain't even thinking about a peace treaty right now,' says Bow Wow, a 26-year-old from Grape Street.

Families were torn apart. During the truce a gangster from the Jordans had a son with a girl from the Nickersons.

'I can't even go see my son,' said 21-year-old Grape Street member Dell Hester. 'I got a baby from a girl in the Nickersons, but I can't even go there no more.'

Not everyone had given up hope though. Twenty-year-old Bounty Hunter Thomas 'Tuck' Graham said: 'We're just trying to get a ceasefire. Just trying to stop all the shootings.'

But the days of peace with Grape Street were over.

'We used to see Grape Street members come over here and we'd give them a pass,' he said. 'But now things are different. I see a Grape Streeter, especially in the Nickersons, he ain't getting no motherfuckin' passes, especially since they killed my homey.'

The homey in question was 22-year-old ladies' man Dwayne 'Sexy Wayne' Brooks. There had always been falling-outs between individual members of rival gangs over drugs and women. But by mid-2005, disputes were being settled with SIG-Sauer pistols and Mac-10 submachine guns. Then the killing of Sexy Wayne marked a return to the pointless killing of someone simply because they were from a different 'hood.

On 5 March, there was a minor conflict in Cerritos at a skating rink, a magnet for many black gang members. Either words or a few punches were briefly exchanged. Bounty Hunters said Sexy Wayne was not even involved in the incident. Afterwards, a group of cars drove to the Artesia Transit Yard near Gardena, where there is a Park and Ride MTA station.

'Shortly before 2am, a group of up to 70 cars that had been cruising just happened to stop there,' says Detective John Goodman of the LAPD's Harbor Division. 'There was some kind of confrontation, and there were a lot of shots fired. Brooks was shot and killed. A lot of people saw it. That may have started the escalation in the current violence.'

Although Brooks was a PJ Crip, he was decked out in blood red following the alliance with the Bounty Hunter Bloods. The man who shot him was thought to be from Grape Street. Even the law-enforcement agencies were surprised by the tie-up between the PJ Crips and the Bounty Hunters.

'The alliance doesn't seem plausible or possible, but that's what we're hearing,' said Detective Dana Ellison of the Los Angeles County Sheriff's Century Station. 'The so-called treaty is dead.'

Other gangsters were also shocked. In Hyde Park, nine miles from Watts – a long way in a gangland that measures its membership by blocks – 45-year-old Kevin 'Big Cat' Doucette of the Rollin' 60s Crips could scarcely believe his ears.

'That's about the craziest shit I ever heard,' said Big Cat. 'The PJs and the Bounty Hunters teaming up against Grape Street. Crips and Bloods teaming up to go at Crips.'

Everybody knew the consequences. With the end of the treaty, payback shootings started up again. If a Grape Street Crip killed a PJ Crip or a Bounty Hunter, then a Grape Streeter must be taken out in retaliation. It did not have to be the shooter who got hit with the payback, or even a gang member. Anyone living in the rival project would do. A week after Sexy Wayne was killed, 19-year-old Jason Harrison was gunned down on 102nd Street inside Jordan Downs. The following day, the Imperial Courts project was shot up. Then the Nickersons got sprayed; then Jordan Downs.

'You can tell the energy level is up in Grape Street,' said Sal LaBarbera, the lead homicide detective for the LAPD's Southeast Division. 'Guys are on guard duty. Trash cans are lined up at the entrance to the projects. Folks are ready to go. Ready to run into their apartments and get the guns.'

Jason Harrison was not a Grape Street gang member. He simply lived in the wrong project.

'Jason was never involved in any of the Grape Street gang stuff,' said Gary Miles, a teacher at Markham Middle School and a long-time friend of the Harrison family. 'He was a good, hard-working student.'

Miles said that a lot of people did not understand how

entrenched people became in their neighbourhood and how loyal they were to their set.

'Lots of these kids are third-generation gang members from these projects,' he said. 'Some kids would rather be a part of the hood thing than go on to junior college or a university if they could. It's that lure. Plus, you throw in the music culture, MTV, and it just adds to the desire. Do I want to be a college football player or do I want to be hood famous? It becomes a seduction.'

Jason's funeral was an emotional event.

'We are here today to take a real good look at our lives,' said his aunt. 'There's been too many deaths on our streets. When a person takes your life, you don't take one life. You kill a family. You kill a community ... Today, parents are burying their children. Kids are killing kids. Children are killing, then going to bed snoring.'

A teenage boy clad in purple started shaking then passed out. Almost no one noticed, not even the three Crips standing directly behind him. Jason's aunt then started to scream. 'He coulda been a gardener, a chauffeur, a movie producer, a cook. We don't know what Jason coulda been.'

Aqeela Sherrills who had been active in the gang peace movement for more than a decade said: 'It's the worst it's been since the treaty in 1992.'

His 19-year-old son, Terrell, was killed in 2003 in an unrelated incident. His brother Daude said the problem was leadership. The Grape Street Crips had just lost their leadership, which cut loose a new generation of young gangsters to go on shooting sprees.

According to LAPD statistics, from 1989 to spring 2005, in the three reporting districts that cover Jordan Downs,

Nickerson Gardens and Imperial Courts, there had been 202 homicides. During that same period, there were 6,470 assaults in the three projects. In 2003, as the situation began to deteriorate, there were 12 homicides in the three projects alone. That same year the 63 reporting districts of the West LA Division had just three homicides. By 2005, killings climbed to ten times the national average. In the projects there was the sound of gunfire every night, but no one reported it unless someone was hit. Soon after the death of Jason Harrison, 19-year-old Keith Moore of Jordan Downs, was shot to death on 105th Street. That same night, Lou Dillon was shot in an area of Watts called Fudge Town.

One of the senior figures in the Bounty Hunters who lamented the end of the truce was Ronald 'Kartoon' Antwine, a 6-foot-4?-inch, 260-pound former menace to society. Back in the 1970s, he would carry a sawn-off Winchester pump shotgun under his black leather jacket and a pistol in his pocket. He robbed people, beat people up and shot them. This earned him more than 15 years in the toughest prisons in California, including thousands of days at Folsom State Prison, made famous back in the 1960s by Johnny Cash. He also spent time in Chuckawalla Valley State Prison – south of the Mojave Desert; this is reputed to be America's hottest prison. A few days after he was released in 1992, the peace treaty was being negotiated, and Kartoon became a key representative for the Bounty Hunters and Nickerson Gardens. One of the biggest sticking points, he said, was that the PJ and Grape Street Crips were concerned about their safety in his Blood neighbourhood.

'One day, I said, "Let's find out",' he recalled, 'and we all started walking through the Nickersons – Bloods and Crips. The young homies were stunned, but they joined in. It was beautiful.'

Kartoon became a community activist and a respected figure in Nickerson Gardens. Official Bounty Hunter historian, he lived at 114th Street and Wilmington Avenue near the Union Pacific railroad tracks.

'You see that field right there by the tracks?' he asked *LA Weekly* journalist Michael Krikorian. 'That used to be our Vietnam. That was the frontlines. That was the border between the Bounty Hunters and the PJs. There used to be weeds higher than me there, and we'd be sniping at them from our side and they'd be sniping at us from their side.'

Despite the breakdown in the truce, the alliance between the PJs and Bounty Hunters had held, for the time being. The weeds were gone and, briefly, the fear of gunfire.

'It's a pleasure to see the people cross the tracks, crossing enemy lines,' he said. 'It's like walking through a force field on *Star Trek*. Used to be, you cross those tracks, you die. Now people walk back and forth.'

But the peace was soon slipping away fast and 46-year-old Kartoon blamed the local government and the lack of resources available for the return of the violence. The treaty's demise had led to a new upsurge in violence by young, reactionary gangsters.

'All the projects are doing their part to stop the violence,' he said, 'but every project has those reactionaries who listen to no one and don't want to participate in the peace movement. All we ask is they don't sabotage the peace. It's like in Baghdad. They got that one religious sect doing all the bombing. But the other sect refuses to retaliate.'

Following the latest round of shootings, Kartoon went into Nickersons with Big Hank, Big Donny and Na Na – other Bounty Hunter veterans – to try to persuade the young homies not to retaliate.

'Our young guys were saying, "Fuck this. We gonna do something",' he said. 'So Hank and Donny and everybody, we had to calm them. It's not an easy thing to do.'

However, he was unable to tell young Bounty Hunters what to do. All he could do was inform them of the consequences of their actions.

'All the guys getting busted, they don't realise what a life sentence is,' he said. 'When the pop goes off, when their head pops out of their ass and they realise they ain't going home after just five years. When they realise they'll never be able to taste a Big Mac or a Quarter Pounder again. To see them go crazy when they hear their moms is dying and they're locked up and can't go see her. When they hear their woman is pregnant by their best homeboy. When they realise they'll never see a night sky again.'

Even though the Los Angeles city attorney imposed a gang injunction against the Bounty Hunters and the Grape Street Crips, making it a misdemeanour for any of them to be together, this was found to be impossible to enforce. Although the homicide rate dropped, briefly, the LAPD had to take a lot of flak over wrongful arrests.

'When gang members are stopped by law enforcement they will say that they are going to visit their grandmothers,' said LAPD Officer Victor Ross. 'But in fact they are just hanging out with a bunch of other gang members, drinking, using drugs, playing loud music, gambling, loitering to be hooks or lookouts. They are doing anything but visiting their grandmothers.'

In the city attorney's report he described a few gang members. One of them was Aubrey Anderson, aka 'Tic' as in 'Lunatic'.

'He is feared in the sense that he is short-tempered and is seen as crazy enough to do anything,' said Ross. 'He is not afraid to commit violence to further the gang.'

Another one is Israel Jauregui, aka 'Izzy'. He has a tattoo on his arm that says 'Kill or Be Killed.'

'He is a violent gang member who is not afraid to commit shootings or other violent acts for the gang,' said Ross.

Izzy has since been arrested by the Federal authorities and Tic has gone underground.

The leader of the Crips at Imperial Court was 39-year-old Steven Myrick, aka PJ Steve, who had 'P' and 'J' tattooed on his throat in letters two inches high. Of the three projects in Watts, Imperial Courts is the most run-down. There were just 490 units in blue and green buildings. Flowers were rare, trash was ubiquitous and packs of young men gave the evil eye to every stranger. PJ Steve was serving nine years for kidnapping, robbery and assault in 1992 when he heard about the peace treaty.

'I was locked up when the peace treaty happened, and I was confused about it for a while. I couldn't get it,' says PJ Steve. 'But then you realise it was a move for the kids. Kids need a better way than the way we had it. But now you got kids going back to the same ways.'

PJ Crip 'Cornbread' chimes in that he no longer felt safe in Jordan Downs. Meanwhile in Jordan Downs, the

Grape Streeters were sanguine about the breakdown of the treaty.

'I didn't really like the peace treaty anyway,' said 29-year-old Scrap. 'If I kill you today, then one of your homies who's like 11 or 12 now is gonna remember it, and when he gets older he's gonna blow my head off. That's what's happening today.'

Kmond Day, nephew of legendary Grape Streeter Wayne 'Honcho' Day, blamed drinking for the violence.

'Alcohol is not for peace,' he said. 'But some people drink cuz there's nothing else to do. The reality is, if we have guys from our own hood who get high and we can't control them here, how can we expect them to go to other hoods and not act stupid?'

What's more, most gang members did not even know why they got involved in the violence.

'A lot of so-called gang members could win Oscars,' he said. 'They're acting like gang members. They're doing the stuff gang members do – shooting, killing – but they don't even know the whole purpose of representing the hood. If you ask them why they bang, they say, "To represent the hood." Represent what? There is no point in representing the hood. What's the purpose? There is no purpose.'

He believed that most kids killed out of fear – not fear of gangsters from outside, but members of their own gang.

'You got cats that's killing cats from other projects, and the homies that are with them are afraid of them, so they try to impress their big homies,' said Kmond. 'But really, they are just scared. But they think it's the only way to survive.'

Others blamed the police, particularly the rough tactics

of LAPD Officer Christian Mrakich. They claimed he harassed people and encouraged the gang wars.

'We have a lot of bad things to say about Grape Street, too,' said Captain Sergio Diaz, Mrakich's commander. 'They are killers, dope dealers and robbers. Mrakich and Ross are very effective in the projects, and of course many people hate them, quite naturally.'

Unlike others in the LAPD, Diaz praised the now-fallen peace treaty.

'There was a lot of scepticism in the department about the treaty, but I believe it made a significant difference in the violent-crime rate,' said Diaz. 'Obviously, the truce thing was good in that people weren't shooting each other. But now, unfortunately, that is over.'

On the evening of 9 April 2005, Officers Darren Stauffer and Oscar Ontiveros, from Diaz's Southeast Division, were involved in a shooting that left Bounty Hunter Spencer 'Fox' Johnson dead. They said he had pointed an assault rifle at them near 112th Street and Bellhaven. The word was that Fox was on the lookout for an attack from the Grape Street Crips at the time.

Another Bounty Hunter, 24-year-old Kemal Hutcherson, was also gunned down on the ironically named Success Avenue – not by the police this time – in the early hours of 9 May.

However, there were peacemakers from Grape Street, such as Bow Wow, who met with their counterparts from the other projects and reported back to their young homies.

'We need to keep conversating,' he said. 'There's a new leadership, and we just need to keep talking and not shooting.'

The new generation of leaders, it was said, were trying to prevent a 15-year-old boy getting into a car with an AK-47 and shooting another black boy, because he lives in a housing project that is similar to his own but has a different name.

'This is not about the Nickerson Gardens or the Jordan Downs or the Imperial Courts,' said Michelle Irving, a former Sybil Brand regular turned gang-intervention worker. 'Those are just names someone gave three housing projects ... It's sad to see a young person walking down the street worried about if he or she is going to get shot. They should be walking down the street thinking about school. Thinking about a future. A bright one.'

But inexorably, gang violence continued to ravage the sprawling projects in Watts. In January 2006 alone, there were 19 gang-related shootings and seven deaths within the Jordan Downs housing complex. By then, one of the potential peacemakers was dead. On 13 December 2005, after over two decades on death row, Stanley 'Tookie' Williams was executed by lethal injection in San Quentin State Prison. During his first years in jail he had been implicated in attacks on guards and escape plots. But after 1993, he became an outspoken anti-gang advocate and author. He was nominated for a Nobel Peace Prize three times. Last-minute requests for clemency and a four-week stay of execution were rejected by Governor Arnold Schwarzenegger. Williams's 32-year-old son, who had avoided the gangs and worked for a social security agency, got a standing ovation at the funeral and rapper Snoop Dogg, a former Crip, recited a poem in Williams's honour.

The neighbourhood still suffers from gang violence and poverty. Joblessness remains rife. Of the 885,000 people living in the 60 square miles of South Los Angeles, there are twice as many Latino residents as African-Americans, and 40 per cent of the residents are foreign-born. Efforts have been made to revitalise South LA, including the construction of new business districts and shopping centres. And in 2008, the homicide rate in Los Angeles sank to a 40-year low – there were 392.

But then one balmy night in August night in 2009, things kicked off again. This time the battle was between the Hoover Criminals and the Main Street Crips. The Hoover Criminals were a big crew in the area. Their turf stretched from Vernon Avenue down past Century Boulevard and into 'the hundreds', as the streets are known locally. They were belligerent and had a hard time getting along with anybody, except the Main Street Crips, who were one of the more muscular gangs in the neighbourhood. They commanded respect as they had money to throw around and even owned their own small record label.

Over the years, the two gangs had carved up their patch of South LA. They settled on Broadway as their loose border – the Hoovers to the west, the Main Street Crips to the east. The two gangs had coexisted that way for as long as anyone could remember, partly out of old friendships, partly because their alliance was good for business.

Then, on 15 August 2009, the Main Street Crips threw a party and invited the Hoovers. One gangster made a salacious remark about another gangster's girlfriend. Guns were pulled. Shots were fired. And an old-fashioned gang war was underway. Soon the body count was climbing.

First came the shooting of 13-year-old Daquawn Allen, a seventh-grader. On 16 August, the day after the squabble at the party, Daquawn walked with a friend to a swap meet where he bought some balloons. On their way home, at 12.20 in the afternoon, in front of a hair salon and a cellphone shop at Broadway and 88th Place, a gunman shot Daquawn twice in the chest with a semi-automatic pistol. He died later in hospital. According to his family and the police, he was not gang member. However, he was born just west of Broadway in Hoover Criminals territory. He never knew his father and, when he was nine, his mother was sent to prison. It was then that he moved in with his 50-year-old grandmother Linda Allen and, while her house was just a few blocks away, it was the other side of Broadway in an area the Main Street Crips considered their own. When Daquawn was killed, his grandmother heard the shots from her living room.

Daquawn was an easy-going boy with impish smile. He was well liked. Privately, his grandmother said, he was terribly upset that he had never known his father. He was desperate for male attention and affection. She said he found it to some degree with the 94 Hoovers, sometimes spelled '9-Foe' and named after West 94th Street. They were a set of Hoovers Criminals and part of the larger umbrella gang. They even gave Daquawn a street name – Four Star.

'I told him, "You use the name your momma gave you",' said his grandmother.

To Daquawn, the Hoovers were not a gang of criminals but a brotherhood. She tried to dissuade him.

'But kids don't listen,' she said. 'They think they know more than you.'

She said she knew the public might think Daquawn was just another gangster.

'People say: "Well, he got what he deserved." But this is family to me. And it hurts,' she said. 'This is the worst it's been for a long time.'

'It's frightening how something so trivial can set this off,' said Sergeant Dan Horan of the LAPD's 77th Street Division, one of two police districts that cover the gangs' territories.

This new outbreak of gang violence bucked a hopeful trend. The LAPD's Southeast Division, for example – ten square miles containing 66 gangs, and another district affected by the dispute – averaged about 140 homicides per year in the late 1980s and early 1990s, when the violence peaked. Officials said they expected to finish 2009 somewhere in the fifties. Now all hope of that was gone as the Hoover-Main Street dispute sat on top of a broader spike in killings across South LA that summer. In July and August 2009, South LA recorded 40 homicides, double the rate at the beginning of the year. On 25 August, Mayor Antonio Villaraigosa and Police Chief William J. Bratton announced that they had created a multi-agency task force to deal with the rise in gang violence. This meant nothing to the gangs. At eight o'clock that night, a gunman walked into the heart of Main Street Crip territory – Main Street itself – and shot 16-year-old Robert Nelson and 29-year-old Drayvon James. James was pronounced dead at the scene at 8.40; Nelson died in hospital 13 minutes later. The double homicide, which has not been solved, is considered one of the incidents that might be linked to the Hoover-Main Street dispute, police said.

'For this guy to do this on foot, up close and personal ...'

said Lieutenant Michael Carodine. 'This is something we haven't seen in a long time.'

On 28 August, the LAPD arrested 21-year-old Kristopher Thomas in connection with the killing of Daquawn Allen. He was charged with one count of murder and held on $1.5-million bail. Thomas, a Main Steet Crip, has pleaded not guilty.

Thirty-nine-year-old Robbie Warren, a former Hoover who served two prison terms for robbery, said the killing was not a gang-sanctioned act but the work of a misguided gang member acting as a lone wolf.

'You don't get stripes for killing a child,' Warren said.

That did not make any difference as it was now open season in the district, besides which other gangs may have contributed to the neighbourhood's outbreak of violence.

'Broadway is a big street,' said Warren. 'You have all kinds of gangs going up and down there. There is no telling who is coming in.'

But the heart of the matter was the tension between the Hoovers and Main Streeters. The task force flooded the area with officers. They were as many as a hundred officers in the streets some nights. Meanwhile, the gangs went underground. The 94 Hoovers even decided to make themselves scarce for their 'Hood Day' – an annual celebration on the day that matches their name. In the case of the 94 Hoovers, it is 9/4, or September 4. Instead of throwing a party in the neighbourhood – inviting both unwanted scrutiny and violence – the gang decided to spend the day 18 miles to the south at Cabrillo Beach, according to LAPD Officer Michael Knoke.

'They know that the heat is on,' he said.

The evening after the Hoovers' Hood Day, Knoke, his partner Officer Jose Gasca and an anti-gang operations supervisor Sergeant Randy Goens went out to check for trouble. Near 89th Street and Broadway, a stone's throw from where Daquawn was killed, they turned off their squad cars' lights and floored it down a forbidding alley full of abandoned couches and tyres. They emerged at a spot that is usually a major hangout for 94 Hoovers. It was a Saturday night, and there was not a soul to be found.

But just because no one was on the street it did not mean the dispute had been settled. The police were bracing themselves for the killings to come.

'It's on,' said Lieutenant Michael Carodine, who directs anti-gang operations. 'It's on. And it's not going to be over until it's over.'

However, in the blood-drenched world of gangland violence there are some bright spots. The Salvation Army community centre on South Central Avenue in South Los Angeles finds itself on the border between areas controlled by the Bloods and the Crips and remains the only building in the area that has not been defaced by graffiti. Even the Virgin of Guadalupe painted on the mini-market across the street hasn't escaped tagging by vandals.

'Any wall poses a temptation for graffiti vandalism,' said Senior Lead Officer Martin Martinez of the 77th Street Division. 'Am I surprised? Yes, of course. But this is a place the community takes pride in.'

Instead, the walls carry a mural by local artist Eduardo 'Lalo' Marquez, showing the services offered inside. Youths from competing gangs play basketball in the centre's gym and work out together in its weight room.

'They walk in the building, they go neutral,' said the centre's director Mortimer Jones. 'And they're playing on the same team. These are the guys who are supposed to be fighting in the streets.'

What's more, the area is attracting tourists. A non-profit group called LA Gang Tours is now offering bus tours of the areas where street gangs such as the Bloods and the Crips hang out.

'This is ground zero for a lot of the bad in this city,' said former gang member Alfred Lomas, who is spearheading the tours. 'It could be ground zero for a lot of the good too. This is true community empowerment.'

Others are cashing in selling T-shirts with gangs tags on them. Kids shoot tourists with water pistols, then sell them T-shirts bearing the legend: 'I Got Shot in South Central.'